Dedication

To all the dedicated people who are rapidly making Tumblr the coolest place on the Web.

S W A	4/13

Contents

About the Author

Bud Smith has written and edited tons of books over the past 25 years, covering a variety of computer topics, including guides to buying a computer, using all kinds of software, and doing almost anything you can think of online. His most recent title is *WordPress In Depth*, a thorough book about the most popular blogging platform worldwide, coauthored with Michael McCallister. Bud began writing computer books in 1984, the year of the iconic 1984 television commercial for the Macintosh. An early success was Que's *Computer Buyer's Guide*, covering the then-latest and greatest in computer hardware and software. He has also written about creating web pages, Android phones, and the iPad. Bud continues to work as a writer, project manager, and marketer to help people get the most out of technology as it advances. He currently lives in the San Francisco Bay Area, where he participates in environmental causes when he's not working on one of his many technology-related projects.

Acknowledgments

The first person to thank is Michelle Newcomb, who brought me straight from coauthoring a book about WordPress to this exciting project; thanks also go to development editor Ginny Munroe, for helping bring the first mainstream book about Tumblr into being; to copy editor Barbara Hacha, for helping to straighten snarled syntax; to technical editor Paul Chaney, for making sure everything said here is true and correct; and finally, to the production team at Pearson, who applied their talents to bring my musings about using Tumblr into the useful and attractive *Teach Yourself* format. Special thanks to James and Veronica, for giving me someone to try to impress with these efforts. Also, thanks to the many friends online who helped encourage me to bring to life a book about one of their favorite tools.

We Want to Hear from You

As the reader of this book, you are our most important critic and commentator. We value your opinion and want to know what we're doing right, what we could do better, what areas you'd like to see us publish in, and any other words of wisdom you're willing to pass our way.

You can email or write me directly to let me know what you did or didn't like about this book—as well as what we can do to make our books stronger.

Please note that I cannot help you with technical problems related to the topic of this book, and that due to the high volume of mail I receive, I might not be able to reply to every message.

When you write, please be sure to include this book's title and author, as well as your name and contact information. I will carefully review your comments and share them with the author and editors who worked on the book.

Email: consumer@samspublishing.com

Mail: Greg Wiegand
         Associate Publisher
         Sams Publishing
         800 East 96th Street
         Indianapolis, IN 46240 USA

Reader Services

Visit our website and register this book at informit.com/register for convenient access to any updates, downloads, or errata that might be available for this book.

Introduction

Tumblr has gradually, well, tumbled into a position of respect, even awe, among people who use blogging tools such as WordPress and Blogger, microblogging tools such as Twitter, and online destinations such as Facebook. Tumblr is a hot site and a new service that has steadily grown in usage and reputation. It's a solution to problems you only gradually realize that you have as you use the new communication tools.

Tumblr serves as a vital intermediary and connecting point between tweets, blog posts, and multimedia presentations, combining the immediacy of Twitter (or an in-person conversation) and the permanence of a well-managed blog. The rules for using Tumblr to its best advantage are still evolving; this book shows you how to get around Tumblr and make the most of it in just a few minutes at a time. By the end, you'll have a tumblog you can be proud of!

About This Book

As part of the *Sams Teach Yourself in 10 Minutes* guides, this book aims to teach you the ins and outs of using Tumblr without using a lot of precious time. Divided into easy-to-follow lessons that you can tackle in about 10 minutes each, you learn the following Tumblr tasks and topics:

- ▶ How to easily set up a Tumblr account

- ▶ How to create and manage a simple tumblog

- ▶ How to choose a theme for your tumblog

- ▶ How to select and use a custom domain name

- ▶ How to keep your tumblog within the Tumblr Terms of Service

- ▶ Finding useful tumblogs

- ▶ How to post text to Tumblr

- ▶ How to use links in your posts
- ▶ How to use HTML code in your posts
- ▶ How to quote other online sources in your tumblog
- ▶ How to post photos and video in your tumblog
- ▶ How to post audio clips
- ▶ How to post by email and from your cell phone
- ▶ How to reshape the look and feel of your tumblog
- ▶ How to add commenting capability to Tumblr
- ▶ How to use Tumblr and Twitter together
- ▶ How to tie Tumblr to your blog

After you finish these lessons, and the others in this book, you'll know all you need to know to take your tumblog(s) with you as far as you want to go.

Who This Book Is For

This book is for anyone interested in learning to use Tumblr effectively. Whether you've never seen a tumblog or have maintained one for a long time, this book shows you how to use each major feature of the site. For example, have you always wanted a home for your Twitter tweets? A place where you can blog freely and easily and readily share content from your own online experiences? How about a kind of staging area for all sorts of media content, which you can then add to a standard blog when you want to? You'll learn how to accomplish all this and more.

Each lesson focuses on one specific topic, such as getting your initial tumblog up or posting video to Tumblr. You can skip around between one topic and another or read the book through from start to finish.

What Do I Need to Use This Book?

Using this book is easy; you just need to be curious and interested in what you can do with Tumblr. To use Tumblr, all you need is a computer, a web browser, and an Internet connection—even a smartphone has enough computing power to do the job. That's all. Tumblr is free to use, so if you have these three things, you're ready to go.

Conventions Used in This Book

Whenever you need to click a particular button or link in Tumblr or one of the other sites described in this book, you'll find the label or name for that item bolded in the text, such as "click the **Photo** button." In addition to the text and figures in this book, you also encounter some special boxes labeled Tip, Note, or Caution.

> TIP: Tips offer helpful shortcuts or easier ways to do something.

> NOTE: Notes are extra bits of information related to the text that might help you expand your knowledge or understanding.

> CAUTION: Cautions are warnings or other important information you need to know about consequences of using a feature or executing a task.

Screen Captures

The figures captured for this book are mainly from the Internet Explorer web browser (version 8.0). If you use a different browser, your screens might look slightly different.

Also, keep in mind that the developers of Tumblr and other tools shown in this book are constantly working to improve their websites and the services offered on them. Owners of tumblogs and other blogs are likely to be improving and adding to their sites as well. New features are added regularly to Tumblr and other web services, and old ones change or disappear. This means the pages change often, including the elements found on each, so your own screens might differ from the ones shown in this book. Don't be too alarmed, however. The basics, though they are tweaked in appearance from time to time, stay mostly the same in principle and usage.

Introduction to Tumblr

In this lesson, you learn about the rapid growth of Tumblr, where it came from, and what you can do with it.

What Is Tumblr?

Tumblr is a blogging website. To elaborate, it's a blogging site intended for short text posts, brief extracts from other blogs and websites, and bits and pieces of media, such as single photos, brief video clips, and short sound clips. Blogging via short posts is called *microblogging*; a blog that encourages multimedia interspersed with text entries and quotes is called a *tumblog*. Tumblr was given that name as a signal of its intent to be the best site for tumblogs. Although naming the "best" tumblog can start an argument, Tumblr is the most popular and best-known such site.

Tumblr has been tremendously successful partly because, at least up to this point, it's free to use. It has quickly acquired millions of dedicated users and claimed more than 50 million unique visitors in one month in mid-2009. Tumblr has also tended to keep its users much better than either traditional blogging sites or Twitter, claiming that 85% of its users post regularly, which is much more than the others. This is not to put these alternatives down. Tumblr, in fact, "plays well with others," as I describe in Lesson 14, "Liking, Reblogging, and Following Posts," and Lesson 15, "Posting by Email, Phone, and Audio." Tumblr has a strong and enduring appeal to the many people who try it. The purpose of tumblogs in general, and Tumblr in particular, is to break free of the tendency of traditional blogs to consist almost entirely of torrents of words. There's a reason the leading traditional blogging platform is called *Word*Press; traditional blog posts tend to be long and wordy, sometimes not even broken up by a photograph. This makes blog posts similar to newspaper and magazine articles, and newspaper and magazine websites increasingly include blogs of this type.

Tumblogs were invented to take greater advantage of the accessibility and flexibility of the Internet compared to the traditional press. Tumblogs seem to have emerged in 2005 when the term was invented. Tumblogs anticipated Twitter, by far the best-known incarnation of this desire for brevity and flexibility. (Twitter is the online site and communications service that only allows text messages limited to 160 characters to be sent. These brief messages are called "tweets".)

Why are people rushing to use Tumblr? Tumblr is very easy to use. The site works hard to live up to its tagline, "The easiest way to blog." Part of the ease of use is because of good software engineering on the site, with many tasks accomplished by clicking a few big, bold buttons. It's also because Tumblr encourages brief posts, so keeping a Tumblr tumblog updated is much easier. Yet the posts are interesting because Tumblr makes it easy to use a variety of media.

Tumblr is also interactive. Tumblr makes it very easy to re-post others' Tumblr posts or other web content. (In the Tumblr world, this is seen as a compliment to the original creator of the content, not as stealing.) It's easy to show approval of others' content through the Like button, explained in Lesson 3, "Customizing Info Settings for Your Tumblog." Tumblr encourages a sense of community, with quick, casual conversations over the backyard fence, and makes the feeling of being connected to others much easier to achieve than the somewhat arduous maintenance of blogrolls and other forms of homage in traditional blogs.

The benefit of posting on Tumblr is greatly increased by the ease of tying Tumblr to other tools and other social networking sites. It's easy to post by email or via purpose-built iPhone and Android apps, as I'll explain in Lesson 11, "Creating a Chat Post." Tumblr can take input from a user's Twitter account or send output to a Twitter account, or both, if you'd like. It's also great for using as input to Facebook or traditional blogging platforms such as WordPress, as I explain in Lesson 14 and Lesson 15. In an online presentation delivered late in 2009, Tumblr personnel estimated that more than half of Tumblr bloggers connected their account to Facebook and/or Twitter.

Given Tumblr's growth and its "stickiness" with users—that is, the fact that users keep coming back to Tumblr over and over—why isn't it as well-known as other social networking sites, such as Twitter and

Facebook? It's still smaller than these better-known sites, and it's a bit harder to sum up in a single sentence than Twitter is, for example. Twitter also appeals to journalists, who therefore write about it; Tumblr appeals a bit more to the technically savvy, who don't have the same access to newspaper front pages. (Don't worry about that "technically savvy" part; this book explains it all for you.)

The use of Tumblr with Facebook and Twitter indicates that it might grow along with these other popular sites. There also seems to be a lot of room for Tumblr to grow internationally, because it's mostly in North America and in English so far.

Because Tumblr is so easy to use, it might continue to steal thunder—and users—from traditional blogging sites such as WordPress and Blogger. As you'll find in building your own Tumblr tumblog, using the lessons in this book, there's power in brevity, in sharing, and in flexibly using all kinds of content and media.

Blog or Tumblog?

The term "tumblog" means two things: any blog that has a strong mix of short posts, media content, and reference to new information that appears online; and any blog created in Tumblr, which is a service created specifically for this type of blogging. The word "tumble" here refers to this sense of ongoing change coming from all directions.

In this book, I use the term "tumblog" in the second sense, a blog created in Tumblr. I assume that your blog also is likely to be a tumblog in the first sense, with lots of short posts and different kinds of media embedded. (It doesn't have to be, but this is what Tumblr does best.)

Tumblr History

Although tumblogs have been around for a few years, Tumblr itself is somewhat new. The company went live in early 2007. It was founded by David Karp, who still runs Tumblr today and maintains a tumblog you can access. Lead developer Marco Arment was the driving force behind the Tumblr launch and has been involved in other interesting development efforts as well, according to his tumblog. He helped Jeff Rock create the original app for the iPhone, a key to Tumblr's early success.

Tumblr quickly attracted tens of thousands of tumblogs from other blogging platforms, many updated via the then-new Tumblr iPhone app. Early users included musicians Katy Perry and Lenny Kravitz, followed by several music labels. The ability that Tumblr gives users to customize their tumblogs, explained in Lesson 12, "Posting Audio Clips," also helped. (Tumblr's tag line includes the words, "Post anything. Customize everything.") Tumblr has grown rapidly ever since.

Why was Tumblr created? David Karp is quoted in a May 2009 *FastCompany* article by Chris Dannen: "Tumblogs don't need all the context of a written post," Karp says. "The context is the blog itself, or the person writing it." The idea is that you read the stream of brief posts, along with the interaction with other tumblogs and borrowings of other web content, and get context from that. It's like a mosaic; each piece, whether it's text, a picture, or a re-post, provides a part of the whole.

Although Tumblr grew rapidly in users, its staff has stayed small—still only 10 people as of the beginning of 2010. This was true even after the company received more than $5 million in investment in late 2009, with two of its investors being shared with Twitter. (That might sound like the sites could end up being combined, but the investors are more likely to want to keep them separate, to get the most value out of their investment dollars.) The growth, investment, and connections—businesswise and functional—with other successful web properties seem to indicate a bright future for Tumblr.

The next challenge for the company is how to become a mainstream property rather than a cult favorite. The company keeps adding features and plotting how to reach a much broader base of users.

Uses for Tumblr

Like most blogging platforms, you can do a lot with Tumblr. However, the following are a few uses that Tumblr seems especially well suited for:

▶ **Simple and easy blogging**—This is what might make Tumblr's popularity take off. Keeping up a tumblog is easier than blogging with long, wordy posts, and is more varied and interesting.

▶ **Interactive blogging**—It's easy to subscribe to other tumblogs, bringing their input into your own. This is a bit limited because Tumblr is not yet that widely used, but that also creates a nice feeling of community among users.

▶ **Flexible blogging**—Tumblr users frequently modify their tumblogs, giving them a unique personality. There are also many add-ins for Tumblr, some of which are highlighted in Lesson 13, "Posting Videos," which allow you to further extend your tumblog.

▶ **Private blogging**—You can keep your tumblog private, and only available to users you name—either as a protective measure while you get it up to speed, or permanently, so it can be shared by a group without outsiders butting in.

▶ **Showing personality**—Tumblr users try hard to show personality through their relatively brief posts and snippets of content. Tumblr is a fun, personal medium.

▶ **Standing out from the crowd**—Tumblr is in a nice position, well-established enough to be easy to use and full of interesting content, but not yet the most popular thing on the block. This insider status appeals to a lot of people.

▶ **Staying up to date**—Tumblr is a great way to keep up with anyone you like, whether famous or just a friend who also happens to be a Tumblr user. It's also a great way to help people, not just Tumblr users, keep up with you.

▶ **Updating Facebook**—As Lesson 15 explains, you can tie your Tumblr account into Facebook. After you set it up, it's actually easier to post to Facebook via Tumblr than by entering things directly into Facebook. Updating Facebook via Tumblr is extremely popular among Tumblr users.

▶ **Updating Twitter**—You can tie your Tumblr account into Twitter. This gives you more power and flexibility than with most Twitter tools. Also, the liveliness and interactivity of Tumblr can then be reflected in your tweets, helping them stand out from the crowd.

▶ **Storing your tweets**—You can use Twitter as an input into your tumblog; you can even use your tumblog entirely as a place to aggregate your tweets. It's actually easier to get at your tweets as a stream and do interesting things with them in Tumblr than in Twitter itself.

Why Everyone Loves Tumblr

Tumblr has a list of reasons that people like Tumblr. You can see it at www.tumblr.com/why-tumblr.

Of course, I can't just let a list like that stand without commenting. The following are some highlights from Tumblr's list and some thoughts on whether they really seem to be as good as Tumblr thinks they are:

▶ **It's free**—Can't argue with this one: Nothing on Tumblr costs money. There aren't any ads, banners, and so on. By contrast, even WordPress.com, the easy-to-use WordPress service that offers a remarkable array of things for free, forces you to pay if you don't want ads. It also charges you to change the source code of your blog or host a custom domain name and for audio and video storage. Tumblr doesn't.

▶ **Hundreds of themes for free**—Another bull's-eye. The competing site, WordPress.com, for instance, limits you to about 70 free themes and even the slightest tweak to a theme costs you.

▶ **Dozens of apps for free**—Tumblr does have a strong collection of apps, including cell phone apps, apps for your computer, and browser plug-ins. This compares favorably to the widgets available for WordPress.com, for instance, but not to the very wide range of plug-ins available for self-hosted WordPress blogs. (WordPress.com widgets are like plug-ins for full WordPress, except they're not as powerful.)

▶ **Use any analytics for free**—Tumblr is not so great on this point. For example, WordPress.com has strong built-in analytics—tools for analyzing how many users have visited—and allows you to use the leading package, Google Analytics, for free. Tumblr has weaker built-in analytics, so you need Google Analytics, which is indeed powerful but quite complicated.

▶ **Incoming and outgoing traffic**—There's nothing like Tumblr for serving as a destination or a staging area for tweets, multimedia content, posts to various blogs and sites, stuff you're looking at on the Web, stuff you phone in (seriously), stuff people email you, and more. It's often easier to send content to Tumblr, which adds it to your tumblog, and then feed it into another site or service, than to send the content straight to the other site or service.

▶ **Responsive help**—Tumblr is new and simple, so help is less complex than with other platforms. In addition, Tumblr has a strong Help Center, and their community ambassador, currently Marc LaFountain, usually answers questions quickly.

None of this is meant to disparage WordPress, nor to promote it as a better solution than Tumblr. Tumblr is easier and more flexible; WordPress is more powerful and more complex. The two also work well together.

I can make a recommendation, though. If you're just getting started in blogging, and you have a bit of time to experiment before committing to a long-term solution, start with Tumblr. It's easier and more fun. A tumblog also works well as a kind of bucket for bits and pieces that are interesting to the blogger, who can then use those bits and pieces on other blogs. Tumblr might be enough for your long-term needs, and if not, you can always use WordPress, having earned your spurs in Tumblr.

Looking at Tumblogs

It's a matter of taste to decide which sites are the best to show off something like Tumblr. However, Tumblr provides some help.

Tumblr rates tumblogs according to a statistic it calls "tumblarity"—kind of like "hilarity" for tumblogs. Just as humor is hard to measure exactly, "tumblarity" is kind of hard to pin down. I try to explain it in more detail in Lesson 16, "Using Tumblr with Twitter." Tumblarity, while intended to be used in a light-hearted manner, does provide some measure of "goodness" for tumblogs. It's also used to drive which tumblogs get displayed on the Tumblr site home page—kind of a "top tumblogs" spotlight driven by tumblarity ratings. You can try to achieve this coveted status, and how to try is explained in Lesson 16.

Here, for purposes of orientation, I'll show four tumblogs I know of and like. You'll no doubt find favorites of your own.

Garfield Minus Garfield

The Tumblr community, known as the *Tumblrverse*, occasionally makes its voice heard on various matters. In early 2009, an unofficial vote ranked the site Garfield Minus Garfield, at garfieldminusgarfield.net as the top tumblog overall.

The topic of Garfield Minus Garfield is simple: Start with the widely published Garfield comic strip, about the interaction between a fat, lazy cat, Garfield, and his owner, Jon, and republish the strip *with the image and thought balloons of Garfield removed*. The result is eerie, a bit like the famous play *Waiting for Godot*, in which two characters spend the whole play waiting for a third character to show up. Waiting for Garfield, perhaps?

This is funny, but what makes it a particular favorite of the Tumbleverse? It demonstrates some of the most distinctive aspects of Tumblr, including the following:

- ▶ **Utter contempt for copyright through reblogging**—People post copyrighted content to their tumblogs freely in the expectation that the copyright holders take this as praise rather than a rights violation. The holders of the Garfield copyrights have taken the former approach, allowing the strip to be altered and republished.

- ▶ **Pointillism**—Pointillism is a painting style in which images are built up by many barely visible dots. Similarly, tumblogs build up an image of the tumblogger through the accumulation of short posts. The Garfield-less strips lead the blog visitor not only to consider the true nature of the Garfield strip and its creator, but also of a blogger who would come up with this idea and carry it out, day after day after day.

▶ **Multimedia use**—GarfieldMinusGarfield is the furthest thing from a text-heavy blog typically found on most blogging sites. In fact, by removing Garfield's thought balloons, it's even lighter in text than the original comic strip.

▶ **(Multi)media savviness**—GarfieldMinusGarfield has become a book, despite the somewhat niche appeal of Tumblr as a site and of existentialism—or, in the case of Garfield in this tumblog, non-existentialism—as a philosophical school. If you become a dedicated tumblogger, you might be surprised to find out who becomes a fan of your tumblog, and even what that might lead to. (See the IBM example later in this lesson.)

Magic Molly

Another winner in the same unofficial vote that recognized the Garfield Minus Garfield site, Magic Molly is a simple, text-led tumblog that somehow strikes a similar chord. Molly Young, the blogger, is a published writer who lives in Manhattan. The blog, shown in Figure 1.1, has a wistful quality, almost a feeling of longing or nostalgia, which is surprising to find from such a young author.

Somewhat unusual for tumblogs, the distinguishing characteristic of Magic Molly is the quality of the writing, achieved in notably short posts—almost a kind of haiku found more often on Tumblr than elsewhere.

Magic Molly is also a good example of how much can be achieved without customizing a Tumblr theme, in contrast to the next example.

Chris Dannen

An example of what can be accomplished by modifying a Tumblr theme can be found at chrisdannen.com, shown in Figure 1.2: the tumblog of freelance writer Chris Dannen. Chris's site is a good example because of the quality of content and because of the ambition of the Tumblr theme changes, which yield a unique result—interesting but not intimidatingly polished.

FIGURE 1.1   Magic Molly is a classic tumblog in a simple Tumblr theme, featuring short but somehow weighty posts.

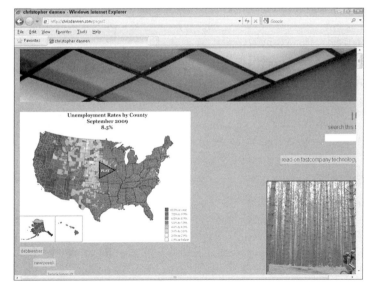

FIGURE 1.2   Chris Dannen modified a Tumblr theme to create his own unique web presence.

Chris's site incorporates a Google map of his location, the ability to chat with him live on Google Chat when he's available, and a regular tumblog, with music videos, photos, and text posts mixed together. However, the number of blogs that follow a clip of failed Presidential candidate Ron Paul with quotes from writer and philosopher Jose Luis Borges is almost certain to be few.

IBM Smarter Planet

Companies have to make use of social media to reach people today, just as they had to advertise on television years ago, because it's where a big part of their target audience is.

IBM's Smarter Planet tumblog, shown in Figure 1.3, is dedicated to a specific initiative of the technology giant: its effort to find solutions for social and sustainability problems.

FIGURE 1.3   IBM has gotten smart about its Tumblr presence.

Many of the posts are simply re-posts of newspaper articles on these themes. The Tumblr theme isn't complicated—not as fancy, for instance, as Chris Dannen's in the previous example. The light touch IBM uses has gotten a good reception on Tumblr.

The point of the Smarter Planet tumblog isn't to shove every marketing message from IBM's worldwide presence through the Tumblr site. It's to pick a specific thing that IBM is doing that fits Tumblr and use the tumblog in the way that best fits this inherently suitable initiative.

This kind of light touch can be hard to come up with in a marketing meeting; it's more likely to be the result of letting some bright person, whether young or old, go off on their own. Personality, creativity, and consistency are important elements for a successful Tumblr presence, even a corporate one.

Summary

In this lesson, you learned about Tumblr's history, what it's good for, and even a bit about its limitations. In the next lesson, you open a Tumblr account and set up your tumblog.

LESSON 2

Signing Up and Setting Preferences for Tumblr

In this lesson, you sign up for Tumblr, review the preferences for your account, and make any needed changes.

Signing Up for Tumblr

It's good to get signed up for Tumblr and make some early decisions before you spend too much time looking at existing tumblogs. By signing up first, you can subscribe to tumblogs you like within Tumblr and add favored content to your own tumblog.

Signing up for Tumblr is easy. Until you sign up, the home page of Tumblr is a big invitation to sign up, as shown in Figure 2.1.

Follow these steps to sign up for Tumblr:

1. On the Tumblr home page, enter the email address you want to use.

   Don't worry—your email address won't be shown to your tumblog visitors based on entering it here.

2. Enter the password you want to use.

   Tumblr isn't as strict as some sites about forcing you to use a particularly complex password. If someone gets your Tumblr password, the only danger to you is that the person could post as you on Tumblr. This could be highly embarrassing, but there's no credit card or other financial information involved.

FIGURE 2.1   The Tumblr home page is somewhere between inviting and overwhelming.

3. Enter the web address you want to use.

Tumblr points out in the prompt for this field that you can change your URL at any time, but be aware that after you share your URL with people and start getting search engine hits relating to it, you'll want to keep it the same if at all possible.

What Tumblr URL Should You Use?

You can use two kinds of URLs for your tumblog: a Tumblr URL, in the form *yourchoice*.tumblr.com, or a custom domain name, in the form www.yourchoice.com.

For a Tumblr URL, you need to choose one that's not already in use. There are more than a million tumblogs already, so this won't be easy. You might need to go beyond normal English words and common names. Consider tossing in some misspellings, digits, or foreign words. Try to keep it short because you and, hopefully, others will be typing it a lot if you don't.

> If you want to eventually use a custom domain name, you might want your Tumblr URL to have the same custom part at the beginning. In that case, you'll need to identify an available custom domain name before you choose a Tumblr URL with the same custom string.

Choosing Your Account Preferences

Before you start posting, you will want to make sure that Tumblr is set up the way you want it to be. You also want to know what your options are for changing how your tumblog works.

Many of these settings are available on the Preferences screen. (Others are part of the Customize area, which is described in the next lesson, "Customizing Info Settings for Your Tumblog.") The following is a quick summary of key changes you can make in Preferences:

- ▶ Change the email address or the password for your account.
- ▶ Edit posts in HTML instead of in a visual editor.
- ▶ Show full-size photos instead of smaller versions on your Dashboard.
- ▶ Show notifications (additional updates, such as new followers) on your Dashboard.
- ▶ Get email notifications for new followers and other activity.
- ▶ Tie your Twitter account to your tumblog; additional settings relating to this can then be modified in the Customize area.

Follow these steps to change preferences:

1. Choose **Account**, **Preferences**. Locate the buttons at the top of the Tumblr window, and then click the **Account** button. From the choices that display, choose Preferences.

The Preferences screen displays, as shown in Figure 2.2.

2. Change your email address, if needed, by entering the new email address you want to use.

You can always choose the email address you use to log in to Tumblr and where you want to receive notifications.

3. Change your password if needed.

You can always change your Tumblr password.

CAUTION: If you click in the Current Password box, even if you don't enter anything, you have to enter your current password if you choose to save any changes you've made in your Preferences. To further the annoyance, after you enter your current password, you then have to enter a new password, and confirm the new password by entering it again. If you don't want to change your password, you can Cancel and not save any of the changes, or you can enter your current password as your new password and then confirm the non-change by entering your current password a third time!

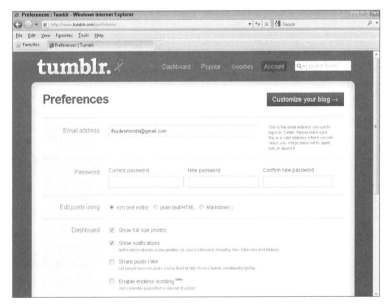

FIGURE 2.2   Tumblr's Preferences are simple and always available.

4. Change how you edit posts; you can use the Rich Text Editor, Plain Text/HTML, or Markdown. The easiest choice is the Rich Text Editor.

The default choice, Rich Text Editor, allows you to add formatting, such as bold, italic, and hyperlinks, to your post using buttons and menus, as if you were working in a simple word processor. The second choice, Plain Text/HTML, allows you to use Hypertext Markup Language—the underlying language of the Web. (When you use the first choice, the Rich Text Editor, Tumblr translates the formatted text into HTML for you.) The third choice, Markdown, allows you to use a different kind of markup technique called Markdown, which is interpreted at the time the page is displayed. These choices are discussed further in Lesson 4, "Choosing a URL for Your Tumblog."

5. Choose whether to show full-size photos or smaller preview versions in the Dashboard.

The default setting is to work with smaller preview versions. You can choose to work with full-size photos instead, which might be slower to download. Full-size photos do let you know exactly what visitors to your web page will see.

6. Choose whether to show notifications, such as new followers and reblogs of your posts, on your Dashboard.

The default setting is to display such notifications, which makes sense for most people. However, you can turn them off by clearing the check box.

7. Choose whether to share posts you like with others.

Tumblr displays a little heart symbol on posts. When you click this heart, you declare that you "like" the post—a sign of approval and an important part of building community on Tumblr. After you "like" a post, later visitors see a notice to that effect on the page. In addition, by default, Tumblr offers users access to a list of posts that you've "liked."

The default setting is to allow others to browse posts you've liked. This can be fun but can also raise concerns about your privacy; you might not want other people to know just how much time you've spent "liking" pages with funny captions under pictures of cats, for instance. You can turn off this capability by clearing the check box.

8. Choose whether to turn on endless scrolling.

    The default setting is to not allow endless scrolling, also known as infinite scrolling. On long pages (more than about half a dozen screens), your tumblog offers users a Next Page or similar button to see long lists of content, which is broken up into separate pages. (Google Search is a commonly used web service that breaks up pages in this way.)

    With endless scrolling turned on, long pages are not broken up in this way; instead, the content is displayed as a single, possibly very long, page. This makes some things easier for the user, because extra clicks are avoided, but it can cause problems with performance of the page. (See the sidebar for more details.)

Endless Scrolling?

Endless scrolling is popular with many people who create web pages—not just tumblogs—because it reduces work for the user who wants to see more content. However, endless scrolling can cause performance problems for a page, or even cause the user's browser or computer to crash. Users are also likely to experience delays in scrolling if they go down through an "endless" page quickly. Endless scrolling also makes it difficult, sometimes practically impossible, to reach the bottom of a page. (Imagine how long an endless page with search results for someone famous, such as Britney Spears, would be!)

With endless scrolling, a user might not be able to reach the bottom of a page, which often includes navigation information and a page's copyright notice. This brings up an interesting question: If a page has required information, such as a copyright notice and links to legal disclaimers, at the bottom, and endless scrolling makes it difficult or impossible to reach this information, can it really have been said to be offered to the user? Just a thought for the legal eagles out there.

Even if you turn on endless scrolling, many users of your tumblog will not experience it because it is not supported in Internet Explorer—the most popular browser on the Web. Endless scrolling also requires that users have JavaScript turned on in their browsers; some users turn it off to disable advertising or avoid potential problems caused by JavaScript. Endless scrolling works on your tumblog only if it's supported by the theme you choose, as described later in this lesson.

9. Choose whether to turn on email notifications for new followers, for reblogs of your posts, and/or for new messages on your tumblog.

   The default setting is to not email you every time your tumblog gets a new follower, nor every time someone reblogs your content. You can turn on this capability and get an email message when someone becomes a follower of your blog, when someone reblogs a post of yours, or when a new message is left on your tumblog. This helps ensure that you keep your tumblog up to date with new content and that you respond in a timely way to what other people do with your tumblog, but it can fill up your Inbox pretty quickly if you have a popular tumblog.

> TIP: I recommend that you turn on some or all of the email notifications to help increase your engagement with Tumblr at the beginning, and then turn off the notifications if the email crush gets overwhelming.

10. If you have a Twitter account and want to tie it to your tumblog, enter your Twitter account information.

    Enter your Twitter username and password. (If you have multiple Twitter accounts, you can tie only one of them to a given tumblog.) You can then tie your Twitter posts to Tumblr, and vice versa, by using your tumblog's Customize page, as described in the next chapter.

11. If you have entered your Twitter account information and want to show Twitter updates in your tumblog's main Dashboard feed, click the check box; otherwise, clear it.

Tumblr displays a warning on the Preferences page: "Only recommended when following a small number of Twitter users." This is good advice, and it means that most of us should keep this feature turned off; otherwise, your Tumblr activity will get lost in a flood of Twitter updates.

12. Click **Save** to save your preferences changes, or click **Cancel** to abandon any changes you've made.

If you click Save, your changes go into effect immediately. You should check that each change you've made has the desired effect; for instance, if you've turned on endless scrolling, try visiting some pages to see what that's like. (You need to use a different browser than Internet Explorer, because it's not supported.) This gives you the opportunity to reverse any settings changes when the results are not quite what you'd hoped for.

> TIP: Tumblr Help is limited, but it's easy to access. Choose **Account, Help**, and then enter a keyword related to your topic. (Don't type it as a question, as the prompt says, which just confuses the Google custom search that Tumblr uses.) If that doesn't work, try using a full Google web search with the word "tumblr," plus your keyword.

Summary

In this lesson, you learned how to sign up for Tumblr and set your account preferences for editing posts, handling photos, and more. In the next lesson, you customize the look of your tumblog.

Customizing Info Settings for Your Tumblog

In this lesson, you learn how to access the Info settings in the Customize area for your tumblog, which are must-have settings for making your tumblog easy for people to use.

Accessing the Customize Area

The Customize area is used to make a wide range of changes that affect how your tumblog looks and works. It's a bit hidden in Tumblr. To access it, follow these two steps:

1. From any screen in Tumblr, choose **Account**, **Preferences**.

2. On the Preferences page, click the **Customize Your Blog** button that displays in the top-right corner of the Preferences page.

The Customize page displays, as shown in Figure 3.1.

Don't worry too much about the look of things in the generic tumblog page just yet; you choose a theme and other appearance options for your tumblog in later steps.

The settings available under the Info and Advanced drop-down menus of the Customize area are the following:

▶ **Info**—Use Info to manage information about your blog: the title, description, your photo, and the URL to access it at a Tumblr URL and, if you choose, a custom domain name.

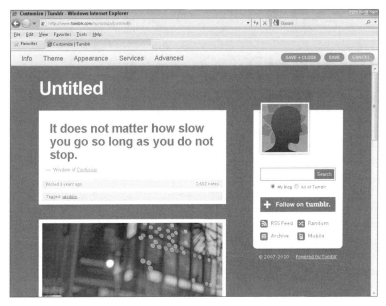

FIGURE 3.1   The Tumblr Customize area is a bit hidden, but powerful.

▶ **Advanced**—Use the Advanced menu to set the time zone, any custom Cascading Style Sheets (CSS) code you'd like to add to your theme, the Post count per page (the number of posts that display on a page), whether high-resolution photos can be displayed, and other options that relate to how your tumblog works.

TIP: Go through the options in the menus described here carefully. They're important, although it's easy to just accept the defaults early on. Later, when something annoys you or you want different functionality, you might not know that an option affecting it exists or how to access it. (It doesn't help that the Customize area is hidden and Tumblr lacks interactive help.) Treat your first trip through these options as a learning experience, and plan to revisit them occasionally to optimize your tumblog as it evolves.

Other menus in the Customize area are Theme and Appearance, which relate to how your blog looks, and Services, which relate to how it connects to other web services. I cover these topics in later lessons.

Changing Information About Your Tumblog

Tumblogs are a specialized form of blogs, and blogs are a specialized form of web pages. The Info menu in the Customize area, which you access by clicking the Info link in the upper-left corner, enables you to change information about your tumblog that applies to any web page, and it includes a couple of options that are commonly found with blogs:

- ▶ **Title**—The title of a web page appears in the top of the browser window, usually followed by the name of the browser being used. For instance, the title of the web page in Figure 3.1 is simply Tumblr, followed by the browser type, Windows Internet Explorer.

- ▶ **Description**—The description of your tumblog is made visible to users in different places in different themes; in others, it might not appear at all. You can include HTML—HTML is short for Hypertext Markup Language, the underlying language of the Web—in your description.

- ▶ **Portrait photo**—Those of us who are camera shy might want to avoid it, but a photo is customary on a tumblog. (If you do not want to use an actual photo, some kind of cartoon or other graphic will do.)

- ▶ **URL**—This is the big one; what URL should you use for your tumblog? I'll go through the options in detail in this lesson.

Follow the steps in the next section to update each of these fields.

Adding the Title and Description

The title for your tumblog should be recognizable. Even though Tumblr windows tend to be wide, visitors to your tumblog may have a lot of programs running on their computer, with many onscreen windows, perhaps multiple tabs in a browser window, and so on. If the top edge of the window and tab with your page are just peeking out above another window, your blog's name should be instantly recognizable.

The description is shown only in some themes. When it is shown, it can be a valuable bit of context for your blog. Because tumblog posts tend to be short, the only other context is given by the look of your blog, plus the accumulated effect of however many posts your visitor chooses to look at.

Many of the posts in your tumblog are likely to be from the others you follow, and your own posts might largely be bits and pieces from around the Web (or around wherever you live your life), so getting a quick but accurate sense of a tumblog's focus can be quite hard. Therefore, a well-chosen description is quite helpful. Consider discussing your tumblog's description with friends or colleagues.

Follow these steps to enter the title and description for your blog:

1. From any screen in Tumblr, choose **Account, Preferences**; then click the **Customize Your Blog** button.

   The Customize page appears.

2. Click the **Info** menu.

   The Info menu is pulled down and displays over the generic tumblog page that Tumblr displays in the Customize area, as shown in Figure 3.2.

3. Enter the title for your blog.

> TIP: Keep the title of your blog short enough that it fits in one line of (large) type across the top of your tumblog—about 30 characters, including spaces. Otherwise, if the title breaks to two or more lines, it's annoyingly hard to read—both where it appears on the top of the browser window and where it appears across the top of

FIGURE 3.2   The Info menu interacts with the generic tumblog beneath.

> your tumblog. A multi-line title also pushes your tumblog posts further down the page, and it's the posts that your regulars are visiting for.

Make the title brief but punchy. It's a good idea to include your name and/or company name, if you can, because this is the most recognizable element of your tumblog—the common denominator for everything else in it. Also, try to fit in a reference to the major topic, theme, or mood for your tumblog, if you have one. For instance, a blog about food could be called Food Stuff; one about the weather could be called Hot Stuff.

4. Press **Tab** to move to the Description field.

> TIP: When you press **Tab** from a field in any menu in the
> Customize area, the Title of the generic blog updates with the title
> you just entered. The title does not display at the top of the
> browser window, but it displays across the top of the blog.

5. Enter the description for your tumblog. You can include HTML
   tags or widgets (which are brought into your tumblog using
   HTML code). Using HTML tags is described briefly in the next
   section, and widgets are described in Lesson 12, "Posting Audio
   Clips."

Just Enough HTML for Tumblr

HTML is the underlying language of the Web. Your web page is created
using HTML. "HTML code" sounds kind of intimidating, but it just means
regular text—just like you're reading here—plus some special codes called
HTML tags. Another name for HTML code is *HTML-tagged text*, which
sounds even more intimidating, so we won't use it.

The following list includes the main HTML tags you might need to get the
effects you want in your description:

▶ <p>— Use the <p> tag to create a paragraph break. The effect is
   to start a new paragraph, which is like pressing the Enter key
   when you're typing on your computer. (If you really want to do it
   properly, put a <p> tag at the start of each paragraph and a </p>
   tag at the end, but a <p> between paragraphs will get the job
   done.)

▶ <b>, <i>, **and** <s>— To add bold or italic to text, surround the
   text with the <b> and </b> tags to start and stop bold, or the <i>
   and </i> tags to start and stop italic. The <s> and </s> tags
   begin and end strikethrough. Here's an example:

   This is a <s>brilliant</s> <b>bold</b> statement that
   includes <i>italic</i> emphasis.

This line of HTML code displays in your description as:

This is a brilliant **bold** statement that includes *italic* emphasis.

Use bold and italics for emphasis occasionally. Use strikethrough to make ironic remarks: "As always, I ~~ignored~~ obeyed my boss's orders." Don't use underline formatting for emphasis on web pages; save it for hyperlinks, as described later in this section.

▶ **Hyperlinks**—For a hyperlink, first decide what text you want to display as the link text—the text someone clicks to go to the page that's linked to. Then surround that text with the <a> and </a> tags. In the <a> tag, include the HREF attribute. The HREF attribute, short for *Hypertext REFerence*, tells the browser where the destination of the link is—what page to display when the user clicks the link.

Adding a simple hyperlink is easier than explaining what it is. Here's an example:

My favorite blogging site is `<a href="www.tumblr.com">Tumblr</a>`.

This displays as:

My favorite blogging site is `Tumblr`.

▶ **Images**—You can easily use any image from the Web in your description, copyright considerations allowing. Just find the web address of the image by right-clicking an image and choosing Properties from the options that appear. The URL of the image appears as one of the properties.

After you have the URL, include it in your description with the `<img>` tag:

`<img href=http://cdn.mashable.com/wp-content/authors/Sean%20P.%20Aune-70.jpg>`

You can also use HTML to create bulleted and numbered lists and indent text, but that's probably more formatting than you need in your description.

If you do want these effects, or want a quick way to get the correct HTML code for the previous effects, follow these steps:

1. Enter the text for your description as a text entry for your Tumblr post—please look ahead to Chapter 4, "Choosing a URL for Your Tumblog," for details. Add all the formatting you want.

2. Go to Preferences and change the preference for your editor to the option, plain text/HTML, as described in Lesson 2, "Signing Up and Setting Preferences for Tumblr."

3. Return to your text entry and copy and paste the HTML code from the text editor into your description.

4. Go back to Preferences and change the preference for your editor to the option, rich text editor.

Figure 3.3 shows the text editor that you use to carry out this trick. This approach will get you going and get you past most rough patches—for instance, when you want to do something a bit clever in HTML, such as adding a hyperlink, but have forgotten the HTML code to do it. After you get the correct HTML code for the initial version of your description using

FIGURE 3.3   Use the Tumblr text editor to generate HTML for you.

this trick, you can probably make further changes to it directly in HTML, using the previous HTML tips and tricks as a guide.

Add a Portrait Photo

Having a photo for your blog is important. Tumblogs tend to be quite personal, and having a face as well as a name to put with your posts is a benefit for your blog visitors.

Follow these steps to add a photo to your blog:

1. Place a photo of yourself onto your computer or the Web. Use a cell phone, digital camera, or any other means you can think of to take the picture. Save the file as a JPEG file.

2. Edit the picture so that it's cropped and resized to a size close to what you need—perhaps up to twice as large, at most. Save the edited photo.

    You can use free tools that might already be on your computer or free online editing tools to modify your picture's size. Flickr, the leading photo storage site, has good online editing tools available within its accounts, including the free ones. (If you don't have a Flickr account already, it's a great complement to a tumblog.)

3. Under the prompt Portrait Photo, click **Browse**.

> TIP: You might want to move the picture you want to use to your computer's desktop so it's easier to find from the File Upload dialog. Alternatively, change the view in the File Upload dialog so it helps you look for pictures better, as shown in Figure 3.4.

    A dialog box, called File Upload, displays to help you find the file in your computer's folders.

4. Find the file you want to use and double-click it to select it.

    A thumbnail of the photo displays in the Info menu. The sample photo in the generic page is *not* updated, but don't worry—the area for your photo on the home page of your tumblog shows the photo when you visit there.

FIGURE 3.4   Find a fun or "cool" photo for use in your tumblog.

CAUTION: When choosing your photo—as in everything you do on Tumblr—remember that anything you post can be viewed by a wide range of people, including your parents and current and future employers, spouses, children, and so on. Think twice before posting content that goes too far in the direction of anything illegal, immoral, or highly objectionable. Tumblr has a free and easy vibe to it, but hiring managers at Fortune 500 companies usually don't.

Summary

In this lesson, you learned how to access and update the Info settings in the Customize area for your tumblog. In the next lesson, you choose a URL for your tumblog.

LESSON 4

Choosing a URL for Your Tumblog

In this lesson, you learn how to specify either a Tumblr subdomain name or a custom domain name to use with Tumblr.

It's All in a Name

Names are important. It's long been said that the sweetest and most attention-getting sound to people is the sound of their own name.

I was recently at an environmental film festival. With more than 100 films showing, at five venues at a time, it was hard to choose where to go. There were only a few film names that were distinctive enough to "pop" out from the rest and yet informative enough to remind me what that film was about. Needless to say, I tended to go to these well-named films more than others.

It's the same with your tumblog. The name you choose for it is important. Your mother, your best friend, and your dog (if dogs used the Internet) can be counted on to go to your blog just because of their interest in you. Other people will probably feel like they have the option to go or not. Having the right name helps you get more visits time after time; it's a gift that keeps on giving. This lesson explains the different ways to get a cool name for your tumblog.

> CAUTION: Tumblr provides little support for creating and using a custom domain name with your tumblog. It's more or less assumed that you have experience with using custom domain names or can

find a friend who does. Alternatively, you might be able to find a
domain name vendor who will walk you through the process. Just
don't count on Tumblr online or email support to hold your hand, let
alone to take care of it for you.

Using a Tumblr Subdomain Name

You have an interesting choice to make with your tumblog: whether to
choose a subdomain of the main Tumblr site as your domain name, such as
myblog.tumblr.com, or to get your own, custom domain name in the form
myblog.com. You'll make similar choices in setting up a WordPress blog, a
Blogger blog, or other types of sites.

Tumblr is often a site that people use with other tools, such as Twitter,
Facebook, Flickr, blogs, and standalone websites. As such, it's often only
one of several elements of your web presence. If this fits you, you probably want to have your Tumblr site be a subdomain: *myblog*.tumblr.com.

The subdomain choice gives you several advantages over choosing to use a
"full" domain name, as follows:

▶ **It's free**—There's no cost to a tumblog, and there's no cost to a
  subdomain name on the Tumblr site.

▶ **It's easy**—Using a subdomain name is easy to set up and
  requires no maintenance.

▶ **You have more choices**—Although a lot of Tumblr subdomain
  names are already taken, many aren't. If you choose to use a custom domain name, you have to find a name that isn't taken.

▶ **It's "cool"**—Usually, it's seen as "cool" to have a custom
  domain name rather than, for instance, a WordPress subdomain.
  However, Tumblr is currently seen as "cool" and distinctive compared to better-known web services such as Twitter and
  Facebook. So, some of Tumblr's "cool" factor rubs off on your
  tumblog, just from using a tumblr.com subdomain for the name.

Tumblr is like a club of individual people who want to express themselves
in this particular way. An example of this is the IBM site at

smarterplanet.tumblr.com, which was mentioned in the previous lesson. There's already an IBM website, but its tumblog is specifically adapted to fit into the "cool" and low-key Tumblr style. However, this is a bit like an elephant dancing, so IBM has to be careful not to be seen as trying too hard and not to associate with some of the more risqué or opinionated Tumblr sites.

Using Tumblr also gives IBM a certain amount of freedom. In a recent tumblog entry, IBM mentioned Google's conflict with China over Internet censorship, the destruction in Haiti, and Iran's election crisis. Normally, a corporation's public affairs department would spend hours wordsmithing such mentions, but on Tumblr, IBM appears to feel free to mention current events somewhat casually.

The takeaway is that even a giant like IBM can choose to emphasize its tumblogs origins by using a Tumblr domain name rather than a custom one.

Using a Custom Domain Name

Usually, you should use a custom domain name when you want to stand out and be taken seriously. However, a Tumblr subdomain already stands out because of Tumblr's own distinctiveness, and it's taken seriously enough.

It's true, though, that a Tumblr subdomain name is a longer "handle" than a custom domain name. People have to remember two things: the subdomain name and the main domain name, Tumblr.com. Having a custom domain name is like being so famous that people only have to remember one name: Elvis. Madonna. Seinfeld. If you want your Tumblr site to be distinctive and easily remembered, seriously consider a custom domain name.

You can use two approaches for your custom domain name for a Tumblr site:

- ▶ Keep the Tumblr look and feel and cross-references to other tumblogs, so the custom domain name doesn't hide the fact that it's a Tumblr site.

- ▶ Heavily customize your tumblog so it doesn't look like part of Tumblr, or doesn't even look like a tumblog at all. This takes expertise in HTML and CSS and in overall website design.

Choosing a Name

Whether you use a Tumblr subdomain name or a custom domain name, you have to decide what name you want to use for the custom part. (For a Tumblr subdomain name, this is *custom*.tumblr.com; for a custom domain name, it's www.*custom*.com.)

Three elements make up a useful Tumblr domain name of either type, as follows:

- ▶ Your name
- ▶ Your tumblog's topic
- ▶ Some element of humor, whimsy, and/or distinctiveness

Using your own name might seem like the easy way out, but it's actually a very appropriate choice for most tumblogs. It's easy to remember and it's personal. It indicates the topic of your tumblog as anything that interests you.

Your tumblog's topic is another good choice, but it's restrictive—what if your interests drift or change completely? Now you've got a bad name—or at least an inappropriate or inaccurate one—on what may still be a good blog.

Adding an element of humor, whimsy, or other distinctiveness to your name or topic—or just being purely humorous, whimsical, or otherwise distinctive—is a very Tumbler thing to do. The whole site seems to take a somewhat skewed view of the world.

Most names combine these elements, because common names, common topics, and even common jokes tend to already be in use as Tumblr subdomains or as web domain names. Therefore, you might need to be quite creative to come up with something truly new.

Here are some tumblog names, with brief descriptions, that might inspire you to come up with your own ideas:

- ▶ **hairbrained (hairbrained.tumblr.com)**—This blog is focused on women's hair. Note the play on words from the old English term, harebrained (meaning, having a brain as small as that of a rabbit).

- **PaperTissue (papertissue.tumblr.com)**—Jeannine is 16 and blogs from Melbourne, Australia. She also has similar names to PaperTissue on Blogger, Twitter, Facebook, and elsewhere.

- **What Would Joan Holloway Do? (whatwouldjoando. tumblr.com)**—This blog considers life from the perspective of Joan Holloway, the tall, red-headed secretary on Mad Men. Note the difference between the blog name and the URL, which is shorter.

- **CopyCats (copycats.tumblr.com)**—This blog introduces its author's favorite cover songs—remakes of popular songs.

- **Genetic Mutations (geneticmutations.tumblr.com)**—A blog of striking photos with brief comments.

- **Sunday Morning (www.sundaymorning.tumblr.com)**—Focus is on black and white photos of old movie stars and so on. A catchy name, but not necessarily a great fit for the topic. (I'm a newspaper nerd and expected something about newspapers.)

- **Stop Nicole (stopnicole.tumblr.com)**—The life and times of a young musician named Nicole.

- **This Machine Will Not Communicate These Thoughts (robertomachinez.tumblr.com)**—A somewhat artistic photoblog.

- **Sweetness (strawberrysyrup.tumblr.com)**—Jessica from Venezuela shares her drawings.

- **What I Wore (whatiwore.tumblr.com)**—Blogger Jessica photographs herself on the way out the door each morning and then lets people comment. A very brave blog indeed!

Follow these steps to come up with a good name for your tumblog:

- Write down your name and variations on it, jokes people have made about it, and so on.

- Write down a couple of likely topics for your blog and variations on them.

▶ Write down some funny or whimsical names and terms, either
  standalone or in combination with your name and/or topics.

Some examples: "goes lightly" is a reference to Holly Golightly in the
famous Audrey Hepburn film, *Breakfast at Tiffany's*; your name plus "after
sundown" implies that your blog is about you, but not your work; your
town or city plus "after sundown" implies that you're writing about local
nightlife.

After you come up with one or more names you like, you can try them in
Tumblr, using the suggestions in the next section, to see if each is available
as a Tumblr subdomain; or you can try it in a domain name search, following the steps later in this lesson, to see if each is available as a web
domain name.

Searchability and Your Domain Name

Since Google offered a big step forward in search engine usefulness about
10 years ago, people have depended much less on remembering web URLs
and much more on searching for what they need online.

You definitely want friends and family to be able to find your tumblog by
searching for your name. Mentioning your own name frequently helps this.
So does including part or all of your name in the domain name. The
biggest help of all, though, is for others to mention your name in their
websites or blogs and then link to your tumblog from the mention. The
more popular the site that links to you, the higher your tumblog appears in
the search terms.

Terms that appear in your domain name are likely to place your site higher
in searches for that term. (This is likely to have a dramatic effect for an
unusual phrase—for instance, if your name is Smeiyth; it's not likely to
have much effect if it's for a hotly contested term such as "software".)

The same is true for terms that appear in your blog's title (which appears
on every page and possibly in links to your site), in the description, and in
the content. The more often a term appears in these, the higher your likeli-
hood of a prominent search engine placing.

It's an open question whether you want to make the effort to make your tumblog accessible via search for any term other than your name(s). It's only good to be high up in search results if the searchers are likely to really want to visit your site—if they click away immediately, no one's interests have been served.

If your site uses the term "cat's pajamas" to refer to things you really like, then showing up high on the list on searches for "cats" or "pajamas" doesn't really help you or the searcher. However, if someone remembers "cat's pajamas" as a theme of your site, then showing up in searches for the complete term is useful.

Think about the terms you want people to be able to use to successfully search your blog. Your name is the obvious choice. However, do you want to include anything else? Search for any possible additional terms using a search engine and try to get a feel for how competitive the term is likely to be. Then, make the term prominent in the name, domain name, description, and contents of your site.

Changing Your Subdomain Name

When you first sign up for Tumblr, you choose a subdomain name. You might have done this hastily; luckily, Tumblr makes it easy to change the name. (Many similar web services leave you more or less stuck with your initial choice.)

However, although the mechanical part of changing your subdomain name is easy in Tumblr, getting people to keep up with various names is difficult. Changing names also means starting over with search engines. Therefore, you probably want to restrict yourself to one subdomain name change shortly after you start using Tumblr, and then stick with what you have. With that in mind, use the following steps to change your blog's subdomain name:

1. From any screen in Tumblr, choose **Account**, **Preferences**; then click the **Customize Your Blog** button.

    The Customize page displays.

2. Click the **Info** menu.

   The Info menu opens and displays over the generic tumblog page that Tumblr displays in the Customize area.

3. Enter the new subdomain name for your tumblog.

   Be sure to completely replace the previous name.

4. Click the **Info** menu name to make the Info menu disappear.

   Tumblr does not tell you at this point whether the subdomain name is already taken.

5. Click the **Save + Close** button to exit the Customize page.

   This is where Tumblr tells you if the domain name is already taken, as shown in Figure 4.1.

What's an IP Address?

An IP address is a unique number for each device connected to the Internet. Though they look confusing, it's the computer equivalent of a home address, which has, for instance, a country, state, city or town, street name, and house number. The address includes enough fields to differentiate a specific residence or business location from every other one in the world. (And if it doesn't, some interesting mix-ups can ensue!)

FIGURE 4.1   Tumblr waits to tell you if the name is already taken.

6. If your desired subdomain name is already taken, repeat steps 2–5 until you find a subdomain name that's available.

Using a Custom Domain Name with a Tumblog

If you decide to use a custom domain name with a tumblog, you should follow these steps:

1. Determine whether the domain name you want—or one close to it—is available.

2. Reserve the domain name using a domain name registrar. (This costs you roughly $10–20 a year; don't pay for site hosting because Tumblr is hosting your site.)

3. Point the domain name's A-record (its IP address) to Tumblr's IP address, which is 72.32.231.8.

4. Wait up to 72 hours for the redirection to take effect. Test this by surfing to your new domain using a web browser; you should be redirected to the Tumblr home page.

5. Enter the custom domain name in the Customize area of your Tumblr page, as described in the following.

There are a few things worth thinking about before going forward. The first is the relative availability of subdomain names on Tumblr versus custom domain names on the Web as a whole. You might prefer a custom domain name that's not available as such, but that is available as a Tumblr subdomain.

Cost and hassle are also worth thinking about. A fee of $10 to $20 a year doesn't sound like much, but over a decade or two, it adds up. You also have to renew the domain every so often, depending on the term you choose to register the domain for (and pay for in advance).

Begin by visiting the Tumblr help page for using a custom domain name. Link to it from the Info menu on the Customize page, as described later in this section, or visit www.tumblr.com/help/custom_domains.

After you secure a domain name and redirect its A-record, or IP address, verify that the change has "taken" by entering your domain name in a web browser. It should redirect to the Tumblr home page.

TIP: The step that most scares off people in getting a custom
domain name to work with your tumblog is changing the A-record,
or IP address, to Tumblr's. Unfortunately, the steps to accomplish
this are different for each domain name registrar. When I registered
a domain name with GoDaddy.com, the largest registrar, they
walked me through the process over the phone. The change "took"
just an hour.

An additional tip is to make sure that both versions of your domain
name work: the version with www at the beginning, and the version
without www. If you aren't given this option during registration,
check your registrar's support area or phone support to make sure
that you have both options. (Some users try each version, no matter what you tell people the domain name is.)

Then, follow these steps to tell Tumblr to send the request on to your tumblog:

1. From any screen in Tumblr, choose **Account, Preferences**, and
   then click the **Customize** Your Blog button.

   The Customize page appears.

2. Click the **Info** menu.

   The Info menu opens and displays over the generic tumblog page
   that Tumblr displays in the Customize area.

   If you need to see the instructions for setting up a custom
   domain, right-click the **Setting Up a Custom Domain** link.
   Choose to open the link in a new browser tab or browser window.

   The instructions display in a new tab or window.

3. Click the **Use a Custom Domain Name** check box.

   The cursor appears in the custom domain name field.

4. Enter your custom domain name.

   Enter your custom domain name without the www.

5. To test your domain, click the **Test Your Domain** link.

   The link opens in a new browser tab.

6. Enter your custom domain name and click the **Check Domain** button.

Tumblr confirms that the domain name is linked to your tumblog.

7. Click the **Info** menu name to close the Info menu.

8. Click the **Save + Close** button.

The Customize page closes.

9. Test your new custom URL in a web browser window.

If it doesn't work—for instance, if the Tumblr home page appears instead—hold down the Shift key and then click the Reload or similar button in your browser. This should clear any cached (saved) copies of the old destination and force your browser to load the new destination.

10. Test the old web address of your blog in a web browser window.

Your tumblog's old web address—for instance, *yourname*.tumblr.com—should also lead to your blog, and the displayed web address should change to your new custom URL.

Summary

In this lesson, you learned how to create a Tumblr subdomain name or a custom domain name to use with your tumblog. In the next lesson, you learn how to change the appearance of your tumblog.

Changing the Appearance of Your Tumblog

In this lesson, you learn how to finish setting up your tumblog, including choosing a theme, changing various aspects of its appearance, and advanced settings.

Changing Your Tumblog's Appearance

Previous lessons described everything you have to do before starting to use your tumblog. After you have your account preferences set up, your basic customization settings the way you want them, and your URL decided, you can start posting and inviting people to visit your tumblog.

Before you start posting and inviting people to visit or at any time after, you can change other aspects of how your tumblog works. This includes the theme, or overall look of your tumblog, many other aspects of its appearance, and specific settings that control how your tumblog works.

> TIP: Other blogging platforms limit your ability to make big changes to the look of your blog. Some, such as WordPress.com, even charge money for it! Tumblr is a great, free, flexible place to experiment with changing the look and feel of your blog, as much or as little as you want to.

Changing Advanced Settings

Tumblr's settings under the Advanced menu are a bit confusing, but worth getting right and understanding, so you can change them if your needs change in the future.

To change advanced settings, begin by accessing the Advanced menu by following these steps:

1. From any screen in Tumblr, choose **Account, Preferences**.

2. On the Preferences page, click the **Customize Your Blog** button that displays in the top-right corner of the Preferences page or click the **Customize** link that displays at the bottom right of the page, above the Cancel button.

   The Customize page, with its generic tumblog, displays, as described in Lesson 3, "Customizing Info Settings for Your Tumblog."

3. Click the **Advanced** menu.

   The Advanced pull-down menu displays, as shown in Figure 5.1.

4. Change settings as described in the following section.

Setting Appearance-Related Advanced Options

Several advanced Tumblr settings relate to your blog's appearance and display in the upper part of the Advanced pull-down menu. Some of the settings display in Figure 5.1. Follow these instructions to set them:

▶ **Timezone**—(Default: U.S. East Coast, GMT-5.) Choose your timezone; Tumblr will use it to time stamp your blog posts, so this is important. You might want to change it when you travel, although that might be difficult to remember to do.

▶ **Add Custom CSS**—(Default: Empty, no custom CSS.) This text box enables you to enter Cascading Style Sheet (CSS) code that overrides code in your theme, if your theme allows this. (The

default Tumblr theme does, but others don't.) The role of CSS
with Tumblr themes is explained in more detail later in this lesson.

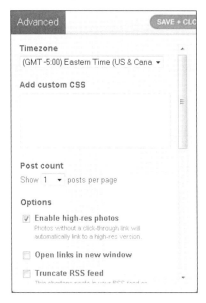

FIGURE 5.1   Tumblr Advanced options are a bit of a grab bag.

▶ **Post Count**—(Default: 10 posts.) Choose the number of posts to
  display in one web page before the user has to go to a new page
  to view more posts. You can choose from 1 to 15 posts; the
  default is 10. The actual length of the resulting page and how
  long it might take to load depends on the content of the posts.
  Because this includes posts from any tumblogs you follow, the
  length of the page is therefore unpredictable.

> NOTE: If you've turned on Infinite Scrolling in Preferences, as
> described in Lesson 2, "Signing Up and Setting Preferences for
> Tumblr," the post count choice is overridden in browsers that sup-
> port Infinite Scrolling and is, in effect, infinite in those browsers.
> However, Internet Explorer, the most popular web browser on
> Windows PCs, does not support infinite scrolling at this writing.

▶ **Enable High-Res Photos**—(Default: Set, which means yes.) If you clear this check box, Tumblr displays a lower-resolution preview photo; if you leave it enabled, the full high-resolution photo displays in your tumblog. Uncompressed photos can easily be several megabytes in size and overfill the screen, so be careful.

▶ **Open Links in New Window**—(Default: Cleared, which means links are open in the same window, replacing your tumblog.) If you want to make all links open in a new window and keep your tumblog onscreen, select this check box. However, this might annoy users who are sophisticated enough to open a link into a new tab or a new window on their own when they want to.

▶ **Truncate RSS Feed**—(Default: Cleared, which means no truncation.) There's an old debate about whether RSS feeds should "give away the store" by including everything or "tease" by only offering parts of a post. There's not much sense in truncating feeds for most tumblogs.

▶ **Use Descriptive URLs**—(Set: Cleared, which means descriptive URLs are used.) With this option set, Tumblr adds a version of your post title to its URL, which makes the URL far more understandable to people. With this option cleared, the description is not added, which makes the URL shorter.

▶ **Promote Tumblr!**—(Default: Set, which means promotion is on.) With this option checked, a Follow button for your blog is shown even to non-Tumblr users. If they click it, visitors are invited to join Tumblr.

Setting Control-Related Advanced Options

The remaining advanced Tumblr settings relate to controlling how your blog works with other blogs and within Tumblr and the Web. These settings include the following:

▶ **Allow Search Engines to Index Your Tumblog**—(Default: Checked, which means yes.) If you want people to easily find your tumblog through search engines, leave this option selected;

otherwise, clear it. (If you're looking for work, remember that hiring managers routinely "Google" the names of applicants—that is, look them up on search engines, in Facebook, and so on. So you may want to leave uncheck the box.)

▶ **Promote Me on Tumblr**—(Default: Checked, which means yes.) If you want Tumblr to potentially highlight your page in its directory or elsewhere, leave this option selected. Many Tumblr users try hard to get this kind of attention.

▶ **Not Safe for Work (NSFW)**—(Default: Unchecked, which means no.) This check box serves as a warning that your tumblog might contain "adult" or risqué content. All it does is exclude your blog from Tumblr's directory and other collections; users don't have access to any setting to exclude NSFW content from their Tumblr viewing.

Set NSFW if you intend to include or reblog risqué content in your tumblog. This setting is not foolproof, even within its limited scope, because content from people you follow might be risqué even if you hadn't intended to include such content in your own tumblog.

CAUTION: Tumblr has a reputation for having a somewhat rough and, well, tumble approach to risqué content. The guiding principle seems to be "we're all adults here," and Tumblr content is only lightly policed. With this prevailing atmosphere, it's easy to end up posting some risqué content of your own, or reblogging someone else's. This is unlikely to be criticized within Tumblr, but might look odd to outsiders.

You can keep the outside world out to a certain extent by not allowing search engines, not allowing your site to be promoted on Tumblr, and checking the Not Safe For Work option; however, if someone emails your tumblog's URL around, or posts it online, some of your friends or family members, a boss, or a hiring manager might take a dim view of the content. Be aware.

▸ **Location**—(Default: empty.) Enter as much location information as you care to. If you're worried about identity theft or other problems, a full address might be too much information to provide. A town or city name is probably safe, and a U.S. five-digit ZIP code might be fine as well.

Changing a Theme's Appearance

You can make changes in the default theme using options in the Appearance menu in the Customize area.

If you change to a different theme, all bets are off—that is, what you can change depends on how your new theme is set up. Each setting in the Appearance menu is turned on or off by each theme. If a theme has not turned on a setting, you won't be able to change that aspect of the theme's appearance using the Appearance menu.

The Appearance menu is great for "quick and dirty" changes to the default theme and other themes that allow it. You can learn whether a given theme allows specific changes via the Appearance menu by looking at the theme's HTML (HyperText Markup Language) with the guidance of the custom HTML Help page shown in Figure 5.4.

Follow these steps to customize the appearance of specific aspects of themes that support each kind of change—your changes show up in the example page as you work:

1. In the Customize area, click the **Appearance** menu.

   The Appearance menu displays, as shown in Figure 5.2.

2. To change the background color, click the color swatch next to the word Background.

   A simple color picker displays, as shown in Figure 5.3.

3. Choose a shade by moving the pointer next to the vertical bar up and down; choose a degree of saturation by moving the circular dot around in the field of colors.

   The color chosen is shown in the vertical bar to the right of the color picker.

FIGURE 5.2   The Appearance menu is a big help with some themes.

FIGURE 5.3   The color picker gives you a lot of options.

4. If you have a hexadecimal code you want to try, enter it in the upper part of the color picker. The other parts of the color picker adjust to show that color.

   A hexadecimal code is a way to specify a color in a concise, compact way. If you want to use hexadecimal codes, one good place to learn about and find them is the RGB Color Calculator at www.drpeterjones.com/colorcalc.

5. When you have the shade you want, click **the Close button** to close the color picker.

   Your chosen color displays as the background of the example.

6. Choose the title, body, and accent fonts from the pull-down menus.

   Experiment to see what looks good. Unusual fonts such as Copperlate Light and Impact are hard to balance with other fonts. Also, not all fonts are supported on all machines, with an especially big gulf between PCs and Macs. So your choices might not look the same on all users' machines.

7. Click the **Upload** button to change the header image and background image.

   Changing the header and background image can change the look of your tumblog and make it more personal. If you do change either or both of these images, consider changing the other settings to complement them.

8. Click the check box to change the settings for Show People I Follow, Show Tags, and Show Album Art on Audio Posts.

   Having these settings turned on increases the richness of your tumblog by adding information to it, so it's unusual to turn them off. If you're trying for a stark, uncluttered effect, that might be a reason to turn off some or all of them.

9. Enter your Disqus shortname.

   If you use the Disqus commenting tool, which you can learn more about at www.disqus.com, you can enter a shortname for it here.

10. Click the **Appearance** menu name to close the menu.

> CAUTION: If you don't close the small Color Picker window by clicking the Close button in its upper-right corner, it stays onscreen even after you close the Appearance menu, hanging around like the ghost of Christmas past. Just click the Close button to get rid of it.

Four Ways to Change Your Tumblog's Appearance

Tumblr offers the following four ways to change the appearance of your tumblog; each of these overlaps in interesting ways:

▶ Use the Appearance menu in the Customize area to change the background color, background image, font, and so on of your blog, as described in the previous section. These settings always work on the default Tumblr theme, allowing extensive customization, but only some of them work on some other themes. (The choice of which customizations to allow is decided by the theme's author.)

▶ Use the Theme menu to choose a different theme from among hundreds of available themes. Then use the Appearance menu to change any settings that the chosen theme allows you to change.

▶ Use the Custom HTML button in the Theme menu to enter your own Hypertext Markup Language (HTML) and CSS, either modifying an existing theme or choosing a new one of your own. This is explained in more detail later in this lesson.

▶ Use the Custom CSS area of the Advanced menu in the Customize area, described earlier in this lesson, to add a block of custom CSS to the current theme. As with the settings in the

Appearance menu, this can be allowed or blocked by the theme's author.

TIP: In the beginning, you might want to see how far you can get with editing the options in the default theme before changing your theme, as described in the previous section. However, part of the fun of Tumblr is messing around with themes, so you might end up doing it yourself eventually.

The Appearance menu and the Theme menu were described in previous sections in this chapter. The next section introduces HTML, CSS, and the differences among them.

HTML Basics for Tumblr

HTML is the original language used to create web pages.

HTML is the text that normally displays in your web page, plus tags that have various effects. It has a fair amount of power but doesn't allow for detailed positional control of exactly where various text and graphical elements on a web page go. Following are a few examples of HTML in action:

- ▶ **The bold and italics tags**—The bold tags—`<b>` to begin bolding and `</b>` to end it—add bold style to text. Text that looks like `<b>this</b>` in HTML looks like **this** when displayed in a web browser. The `<i>` and `</i>` tags work the same way for italics.

- ▶ **The image tag**—To insert an image into a web page, put in the image tag and a link to where on the Web the image is. For example, use `<img href="www.google.com/intl/en_ALL/ images/logo.gif">` to insert the Google logo in your web page.

- ▶ **Hyperlinking**—To make text a hyperlink, surround it with the `<a>` and `</a>` tags, including the destination of the link. For example, with the following `<a href="www.sardis.com">my favorite restaurant</a>`, the words "my favorite restaurant" display underlined and in the link color, usually blue; clicking the link takes you to the website for Sardi's restaurant in New York City.

You can learn much more about HTML from many websites, books, and people you might know from whom you can learn it. It's too large of a topic to be covered in this book.

CSS in Tumblr

CSS is a clever way to allow specific formatting of web content, such as fonts, text size, the location of the various elements on a web page, and more. If you don't already know CSS, you can learn a great deal about it from websites, books, and by experimenting in Tumblr.

HTML and CSS can be used to create a page layout into which new content—your tumblog postings—is more or less "poured." In Tumblr, this kind of page layout is called a theme.

You can access the HTML and/or CSS—they're often used in combination—that make up any of the themes in Tumblr and modify them. You can also create a whole new theme of your own.

Modifying and creating themes is a great "sandbox" for experimenting with and even learning HTML and/or CSS. However, creating a page layout that can support the pouring in of new tumblog postings, and never break—that is, get rendered as an unrecognizable mess—is not easy. Even themes available to you within Tumblr can break occasionally.

A useful page in Tumblr's Help area introduces the topic of creating a custom HTML theme, including the specifics of how various elements work with Tumblr, in some detail. It's shown in Figure 5.4 and is available at www.tumblr.com/docs/custom_themes.

This Help page is fairly advanced, but if you're bright and brave, you can get pretty far with it.

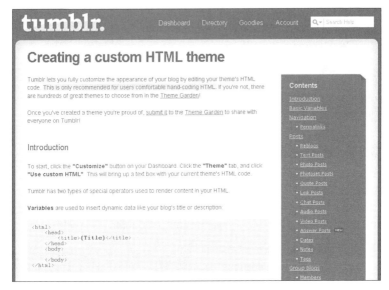

FIGURE 5.4   Tumblr gives you a leg up in theme editing.

Choosing a New Theme

Choosing a new Tumblr theme is easy, from a mechanical point of view. The difficult part is choosing from among the hundreds of available themes and deciding whether to take an existing theme as is, or add your own tweaks to it.

TIP: Even if you're new at this, you might be able to choose a few simple aspects of a theme, such as the background image, color, and so on—either because the theme lets you change these directly in the Tumblr Appearance menu in the Customize area, or by going in and changing the HTML and CSS directly.

CAUTION: Fooling around with the HTML and CSS in your theme could possibly lead to the loss of your entire tumblog and its contents. The situation should be recoverable by switching from a broken theme to a different theme, or the default Tumblr theme, but I wouldn't bet a few hundred posts on it. Consider creating a new tumblog and experimenting with theme changes there before committing a lot of valuable posts to a new, unproven theme.

Follow these steps to choose a new theme for your tumblog:

1. In the Customize area, click the **Theme** menu.

   A selection of about 40 themes displays, as shown in Figure 5.5. You can choose one directly. Simple themes, such as the Easy Reader theme in Figure 5.5, are the easiest to customize, but you might not know where to make changes to liven it up. A theme that's close to what you want, but that has the wrong picture or color scheme, might be easy to modify.

FIGURE 5.5   Tumblr's Theme menu includes a few dozen themes.

2. Choose a theme from the ones available, or scroll to the bottom and click the **Browse More Themes** button.

If you click **Browse More Themes**, the Theme Garden displays, as shown in Figure 5.6.

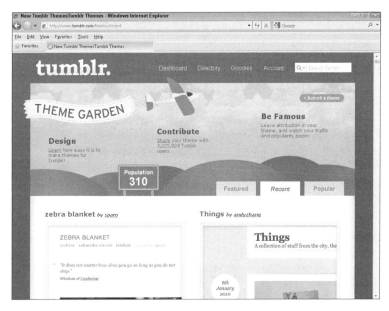

FIGURE 5.6   The Theme Garden includes hundreds more themes.

3. To examine the Theme Garden, click the **Featured**, **Recent**, and **Popular** tabs.

Each theme shows how many people are using it from among Tumblr's millions of users.

4. Click a theme from directly under the Theme menu, or in the Theme Garden, to choose it.

A list of additional themes from the same theme creator, if any, displays.

5. To preview the theme with your content, click **Preview** (I recommend previewing before making a selection).

See how the theme looks with your content.

6. To put the theme into effect, click Install Theme.

Your tumblog now uses the selected theme.

Customizing a Theme

Starting to customize a theme is easy. The tricky part is stopping!

Follow these steps to customize a theme for your tumblog:

1. Choose a theme, as described in the previous section.

2. In the Customize area, click the **Theme** menu.

3. Scroll to the bottom of the Theme menu and click the **Use Custom HTML** button.

The HTML and CSS code for your theme displays, as shown in Figure 5.7. To see the Help page for HTML shown in Figure 5.4, click **Theme Docs**.

4. Make changes to the HTML and CSS for your theme. To preview the pages, click **Update Preview**.

The preview beneath your theme is updated.

5. Continue making changes until you're happy with the result.

6. Copy and paste your HTML and CSS into a document using Windows Notepad or any other text editor; then save it so you have a copy.

You can get a free text editor for your specific type of computer on sites such as CNET's Download.com.

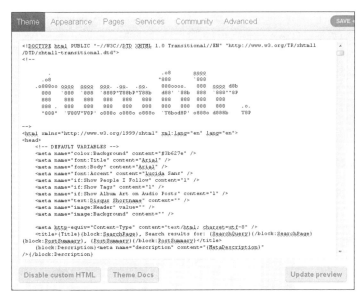

FIGURE 5.7   HTML and CSS code are behind your Tumblr theme.

7. Click the **Theme** menu to hide the customized HTML.

You can continue using the changed HTML as long as you like.

Colors in Web Pages

Colors for web pages are sometimes specified by words, which gives you a limited choice, but more often by an odd kind of number called a hex code, short for hexadecimal codes. A hex code for a web color is six digits, and each digit can be either the usual 0–9 or the letters A–F, with A representing 10, B representing 11, and so on. Each position is a power of 16.

Colors are specified in Red, Green, Blue (RGB) order, two hexadecimal digits per color. So, the hex code #FFFFFF (the # indicates a hex code) means "full red, full green, full blue." You might remember from science or art class that turning up all the colors all the way results in white.

You don't really need to know more than that; just use the simple color picker in the Tumblr Appearance menu in the Customize section described earlier in this lesson, or look up "color picker" in a web search engine and find a tool that lets you choose a color using sliders or knobs and gives you the RGB hex code of the color you choose. Then you can put it into your HTML or CSS, or even into the color picker in the Appearance menu, to specify a color.

That's just the mechanical part, though. The art of choosing useful color combinations is, well, an art! That's the fun part, but don't expect to find the best color combination for your blog quickly.

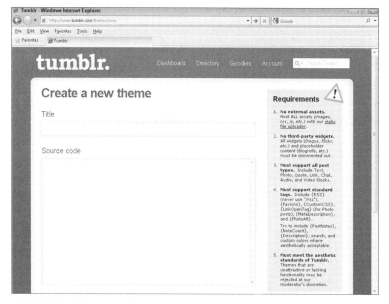

FIGURE 5.8 You can submit your Theme to Tumblr's Theme Garden.

If you think you've created a good theme, go to the Theme Garden, as described in the previous section. (Going to the Theme Garden loses any unsaved changes to your custom HTML, which is why it's always good to save your custom work first.) In the Theme Garden, click the **Submit a Theme** button to upload your theme for consideration by the gurus at Tumblr. The submission screen is shown in Figure 5.8. Note the admonition: "Themes that are unattractive or lacking functionality may be rejected at our moderator's discretion."

Summary

In this lesson, you learned how to take advantage of Tumblr's extensive range of prebuilt themes and its even more extensive customization capabilities. You can make your tumblog do almost anything you can imagine a web page doing.

LESSON 6

Creating a Text Post

In this lesson, you learn how to create a text post in Tumblr.

The Vital Role of Text in Tumblogs

In contrast to most blogging software, Tumblr is great for all sorts of multimedia. However, text is still crucial to most tumblogs. Creating interesting, fun, and useful text posts is crucial to making your tumblog interesting. Even photoblogs, for instance, benefit from a few well-chosen words accompanying each photo. (Many photoblogs and illustrations in tumblogs have text integrated into them graphically.)

This lesson also describes some of the fields that are common to all posts: instantaneous or delayed publishing, tags, and custom post URLs.

Tumblr makes it easy to create plain text and HTML-formatted text posts and include pictures with your text posts. You can create a photoblog without ever using the Post a Photo button. Posting photos is described in the next lesson.

TIP: Tumblr is heavily influenced by Twitter, and the best tumblogs seem to favor economy of expression. Even longer posts in many tumblogs are made up of short paragraphs with plenty of white-space. (One posting in a tumblog says of Tumblr blogs, "the copy is succinct and genuine.") If you want your tumblog to fit in, think about how to keep your postings, and each individual comment within a posting, short.

Adding a Text Post

Take the time to work through all the fields carefully as you create your first text post. The key elements are the title, which gives a label to your post; the body of the post, which is text with HTML-supported formatting; and tags for people searching on the post. (Tags also serve as sometimes ironic, self-commentary on the content of the post. For instance, tagging your own posting "propaganda" is a way of making a joke, while also perhaps being accurate.)

Follow these steps to create the body of the post:

1. From the Tumblr Dashboard, click the **Text** button.

The Add a Text Post screen displays, as shown in Figure 6.1.

FIGURE 6.1   You'll be adding many text posts in Tumblr.

2. Enter the title of the post under the Title prompt.

Make the title of your post brief, include any keywords you'd like to be available for people using a search engine, and note that irony is appreciated in the Tumblr environment.

3. Move the cursor down into the Post area and enter words for the post. Press **Enter** to start a new paragraph.

After you enter words, you can publish at any point. You can also format the post, add tags, and set a later publication date, which are all described later in this lesson.

4. When you're finished, click **Preview** to review the post.

The post displays in a new tab in your tumblog, looking as it would when published, as shown in Figure 6.2.

FIGURE 6.2   It's easy to see previews of your posts.

5. To close the preview, close the tab it resides in.

You return to the editing window.

6. To publish the post, click **Create Post**.

The post displays in your tumblog. You can always revise it later, as described in the following section.

Formatting a Post's Content

Tumblr makes a simple what you see is what you get (WYSIWYG) editor available for text posts. This is like a simple version of a standard word processor, such as Microsoft Word.

What You See Is What You Get

Back in the 1960s, "what you see is what you get" was a line used by a famous cross-dressing comedian named Flip Wilson. Early word processors of the 1970s and 1980s required that users "mark up" text with visible characters to indicate formatting, such as ^B to indicate bolding. When more complex word processors were able to actually show effects like bolding in place, the logical thing to call them was "what you see is what you get," or WYSI-WYG, word processors.

Because HTML was invented in the 1990s, the term WYSIWYG has been used for HTML editors that show the effects of editing "live," like the newer word processors. By contrast, text editors show the HTML markup symbols directly, such as <b> to start bolding and </b> to end it.

Like many modern HTML editors, Tumblr allows users to switch between WYSIWYG mode and plain-text mode.

Tumblr's WYSIWYG editor supports the standard formatting commands available in HTML:

- ▶ **Bold and italic**—You can format specific words or characters with **bold** or *italic* formatting. Use these effects sparingly, but do use them.

- ▶ **Strikethrough**—You can format specific words or characters with ~~strikethrough~~ formatting. This is often used to ironic effect in blogs.

- ▶ **Bulleted lists and numbered lists**—Bulleted lists (like this one) and numbered lists are great for breaking up blocks of text, and they enable you to use fewer words.

- ▶ **Indenting and outdenting**—Indenting is useful for indicating quoted text. Outdenting is simply a way to reverse indenting.

▶ **Insert an image**—This command allows you to insert an image. However, the image must be uploaded to Tumblr first. The uploading and inserting process is described in the next lesson.

▶ **Insert or remove a hyperlink**—You can link any text or image to any web destination.

▶ **Spell check**—Tumblr users tend to be fairly literate, so don't hesitate to use the spell checker.

▶ **Insert a More link**—A More link is not part of HTML but has been more or less standardized for use in blogs. A More link causes everything above it to be displayed on the main page of a blog. To see the full entry, the user has to click More, or a similar word, for the full post to display on its own page.

▶ **Open a text editor**—You can open a separate window that displays the post in plain text, with HTML tags showing. This is described in detail in a later section in this lesson.

Figure 6.3 shows an example of text in the Tumblr text editor, with most of the options in use. Experiment with all the options available in the Tumblr text editor. Mastering them will greatly improve your posts.

FIGURE 6.3   WYSIWYG editing can accomplish a lot.

Adding Links to a Post

One of the great advantages of Tumblr is its capability to incorporate content from all over the Web. One basic, but sometimes overlooked, way to do this is through simple hyperlinks, which are also available in any web page.

Follow these steps to create a hyperlink in the WYSIWYG editor:

1. Enter some text in the text editor.

2. Select the text that you want to serve as the hyperlink text.

   The current trend is to use brief chunks of text for hyperlinks.

3. Under Post, in the toolbar, click the Insert/Edit Link button.

   The Link dialog box opens; a filled-in example of the Link dialog box is shown in Figure 6.4.

FIGURE 6.4   Think, then link.

4. Enter the URL of the destination of the link in the Link dialog box.

   To get the URL, open the web page in a separate browser window or browser tab. Then copy and paste the URL from the browser.

5. Enter a title for the link in the Link dialog box.

The link title displays as mouse-over text, so when users move their cursors over the link, the mouse-over text indicates the link's destination or purpose.

6. Choose a target for the link—the same window or a new window. Click **Insert** to create the link, or click **Cancel** to cancel it.

The target for a link is usually the same window as the link, so that the current window updates to show the Web page that's been linked to. However, you can also choose the option Open Link in a New Window. If you choose this option, clicking the link opens a new window, with the link destination as the URL. Your tumblog is still onscreen.

You can do a great deal with links. Beyond linking to various web pages in context, you can create lists to favorite destinations, to pages in support of both sides of an argument, or for other interesting purposes.

Using HTML in a Posting

Tumblr allows you to use your HTML and CSS knowledge in all kinds of ways—even to learn HTML and/or CSS through experimentation with your tumblog. You can use this knowledge to change the appearance of your entire tumblog, as described in Lesson 5, or just within a posting, as described here.

One way in which Tumblr does this, which is also offered by other blogging and web page creation tools, is to allow you to work directly in HTML.

To work directly in HTML, in the Preferences area, change the mode for editing posts from rich text editor, the default, to plain text/html, as described in Lesson 2, "Signing Up and Setting Preferences for Tumblr." The text editing area changes.

The commands available are fewer and include only bold, italic, strikethrough, and creating a link. Clicking one of these buttons inserts the relevant HTML directly into the text, as shown in the figure. To put other commands into effect, you have to type the relevant HTML in yourself.

I won't go through this in detail here, because it duplicates the effects available in WYSIWYG mode. However, it's worth experimenting with if you want to learn HTML. You can use WYSIWYG mode to insert commands and HTML mode to see what the resulting HTML code looks like.

HTML mode is necessary for solving some kinds of problems and achieving some HTML effects that are not available from the commands in WYSIWYG mode. (These effects might not work in all browsers, because they might be newer or nonstandard.)

Adding Tags to Posts

Tagging posts gives you a way to make your post searchable on terms you dictate, by associating them directly with your posts. This makes it easier for people to find your postings on topics that they care about. It can even help you to find your own, older posts!

You can add tags to any post, not just text posts. In fact, tags are more important for pictures and other kinds of Tumblr posts than they are for text posts, because pictures—while they may be worth a thousand words— don't contain any. Your text post is likely to already include many of the terms that you would normally use as tags, whereas a graphical post won't have words; only tags make the other kinds of posts searchable by a text search.

Ideally, the tag terms are either terms already found in your post or synonyms for those terms. For instance, if your post mentions the Chargers football team in an off-hand way, you could add tags like "San Diego" and "football." You could also add "Chargers" to emphasize it.

> TIP: To strongly emphasize a term for searchability, consider doing some or all of the following:
> - ► Use it at least once in your post.
> - ► Use it in the title of your post.
> - ► Use it in the custom URL for your post (see the section on custom URLs later in this lesson).
> - ► Use it and different versions or even misspellings of it as tags for your post.

This way, if people search for "San Diego sports teams" or "football teams," they'll get your post, even though they didn't include the term "Chargers."

To enter tags, add them in the Tags area next to your post, separated by pressing Enter. (That way "San Diego" comes out as a single term.) Although it might seem like too much trouble at the time that you're creating a post, you and others will benefit from being able to retrieve relevant posts down the road.

Figure 6.5 shows the Tumblr Add a Text Post page with tags added.

FIGURE 6.5   Tags make your posts easy to find.

> NOTE: Other blogging tools allow you to put your posts in categories, which are rigid structures that are set up separately. Categories might be a bit too much structure for Tumblr, which tends to be loosely organized.

Additional Options for All Posts

Besides the many options discussed up to this point, Tumblr gives you some additional choices for yours posts: different ways or times to publish, a semi-custom URL, and the option to allow people to respond to your posts.

Setting the Post Date

Use Publish Now menu to change the post date—that is, the date on which a post will show as being published. You can do this to make posts appear in an order that you determine, rather than in order of their actual post date.

Choose the appropriate option and, if necessary, change the publish time. Options include the following:

- ▶ **Publish Now**—The post is published immediately.

- ▶ **Add to Queue**—Publishes after posts that were previously created and marked for later posting.

- ▶ **Publish On**—This option prompts you for a date and time in the future; the post will be published when the specified date and time are reached.

- ▶ **Save as Draft**—This option holds the post, unpublished.

- ▶ **Private**—Publishes the post, but hides it from visitors.

Setting a Custom Post URL

Normally, the URL for a posting includes a number assigned by Tumblr. You can semi-customize the URL by entering text describing the posting. The post is still given a number by Tumblr, but the custom post URL you enter is added to the number to create a complete URL.

Allowing People to Respond to a Post

Twitter has long been famous for not allowing comments, unlike many other blogging sites, which actively encourage them. If you select the Let People Answer This check box, a form is appended to your post. The form allows people to comment on the post.

The advantages of allowing people to comment on your posts—and the reason most blogging sites have long allowed comments—include an increased feeling of participation by your users and increased amounts of information and opinion made available within the comments themselves.

The disadvantages mainly have to do with a loss of control. When comments aren't allowed, you have control of the entire user experience on your tumblog. You can create exactly the effect you want, without the risk of a commenter distracting from it.

Whether you allow comments or not depends on your own personal taste. You might want to try allowing comments, see how you like the results, and then disallowing them if that seems like the right thing to do.

> CAUTION: Responding to a post is an experimental feature at this writing. It might be withdrawn or changed in future versions.

Summary

In this lesson, you learned specific options for text posts, including the use of WYSIWYG formatting, HTML tags, and general options that apply to text posts and other kinds of posts, such as tags, delayed publishing, and custom URLs.

LESSON 7

Adding Photos to a Text Post

In this lesson, you learn how to create Tumblr-ready photos and add them to your tumblog text posts.

The Art of Photos in Tumblogs

Photos and other static graphics have two important roles in blogs: as illustrations for text posts and as the central point of a post. In Tumblr, photos are particularly important. They often stand on their own, with little or no comment.

The Tumblr community tends to value a certain terseness and precision, in words and in pictures. The trick is to be creative and distinctive in relatively few words, or with just one picture. Many of the photos in tumblogs are quite striking, and others make up an interesting juxtaposition with the accompanying text or other media.

You can certainly use Tumblr for your holiday snaps and so on. However, this is not how the most-visited tumblogs do things. If you want to participate fully in the Tumblr community, you'll use a site like Flickr to host the mass of your photos and be a bit selective about what you put on Tumblr. Seeing the quality of some of the images highlighted on Tumblr might even encourage you to go out and take more and better photos.

NOTE: I use the word "photo" here as a generic term that includes nonphotographic digital images. Many such images have much lower storage requirements than digital photos, and most are better compressed using PNG or GIF, described in the next section, rather than the JPEG standard, which was designed expressly for photos.

To make the most of your tumblog or of any photo storage and posting you do on the Web, it's best to know a few basics about digital photos. This lesson introduces these basics and then shows you how to use photos in Tumblr.

Digital Photo Basics

There are four ways to make digital photos suitable for the Web, and three primary issues for web photos. The four main ways to create digital photos are the following:

▶ Scanning a printed photo

▶ Taking a photograph with a standalone digital camera

▶ Taking a photograph with a digital camera integrated into a cell phone

▶ Using an existing image already available online

The three primary issues that affect all digital photos to varying degrees are file size, display size, and image quality.

File Size and Digital Photos

Digital photos tend to have large file sizes—at least 1MB in size, up to 10MB or more. If they are not compressed, these images load slowly on web pages, and several of them on a page might slow or even halt a page-loading process on some PCs. It's common for the page creator to use a fast PC and a fast web connection that masks the effect, but some users will suffer from problems using the page.

As a result, it's important to check the size of images before uploading the image to the Web. Tumblr automatically creates a lower-resolution preview image, but some users have changed their settings to display large images directly. Other users have set their pages to display unlimited numbers of posts; in that case, even reasonably sized images, in sufficient numbers on a page, can bog down their computer.

It's important, therefore, that you create a smaller, compressed version of your file, appropriate for web display on your Tumblr page. JPEG compression is marvelous for reducing file sizes without greatly affecting image quality. However, repeated, or overly severe, JPEG compression can cause image quality to degrade noticeably.

Use a graphics program to compress your files before uploading them to your Tumblr page. Windows computers come with a simple image manipulation program, Paint, that can do some jobs, and freeware and shareware platforms are available from sites like CNET's Download.com. Flickr, shown in Figure 7.1, and other photo storage programs, as well as some task-specific sites, include image-editing capabilities.

FIGURE 7.1   Flickr includes basic image-editing capabilities.

Display Size and Image Quality

In addition to file size, the other issues are display size and image quality. The display size of an image often has a misleading relationship to its file size. It's quite possible to display an image with a very large file size— that could display with good quality at a size much larger than a computer screen can accommodate—in a relatively small display size. This effectively wastes most of the file size, bogging down page loading with no benefit to the user.

The final issue is image quality. This has two aspects: technical quality, the degree to which an image is degraded in compression, and artistic quality, based on subjective factors such as lighting and composition.

The following is a brief list of image sizes and storage requirements that you might consider using as a reference for your online images. These sizes are for an image with light JPEG compression, allowing about one byte of storage for each pixel of the image. In many cases, you can compress an image much more than that without visibly affecting the image quality:

- ▶ 100x100 pixels: 10KB

- ▶ 200x200 pixels (about a quarter of a screen tall on a typical laptop): 40KB

- ▶ 300x300 pixels: 90KB

- ▶ 400x400 pixels (about half a screen tall on a typical laptop): 160KB

- ▶ 500x500 pixels (more than half a screen tall on a typical laptop): 250KB

- ▶ 800x800 pixels (a full screen tall on a typical laptop): 625KB

Examples of images representing 100, 200, and 500 square pixels are shown in Figure 7.2. As you can see, there's little reason to have an image more than 1MB in size in your tumblog, even using a very large display size and very high quality.

FIGURE 7.2   Match image display size and compression for best results.

TIP: Applying JPEG compression repeatedly tends to intensify the relatively minor artifacts (small areas of visual "noise") that occur the first time the image is compressed. Each time you try a different degree of JPEG compression on an image, start with the original, rather than applying JPEG compression several times to an image.

It's difficult to create an image with good technical or artistic quality with a cell phone camera. Although the number of megapixels available in cell phone cameras is increasing, they tend to lack good lenses, sufficient flash (if any), or add-on lenses.

The iPhone, in particular, has apps available that can help with some of these issues, and careful attention to detail can help. However, people who care that much about their photos tend to use better cameras. So, cell phone pictures are usually not as good as those taken with standalone digital cameras.

When preparing photos for Tumblr, try to start with interesting original images with reasonable artistic and technical quality. Then change their display size and compression ratio in tandem so you create a technically high-quality image with a reasonable file size.

Using Online Photos

There are two ways to use online photos in Tumblr. One is by reblogging someone else's photo posts. This is a well-respected practice in tumblogs, and many interesting tumblogs are simply streams of others' pictures. The other way is by getting the URL to a photo and then including that URL in your tumblog. Tumblr displays the photo in your blog as if you had uploaded it yourself.

When the photo is displayed in your blog, it's actually transferred from the host's server to the user's computer. This does cause some minor cost to the host of the photo. However, bandwidth is cheap enough these days that this seems to be a concern only in cases where some combination of the following occur: The photo has a large file size, the host has a strict bandwidth limit, and/or a page that "borrows" a photo in this way is very popular.

In addition to file size, the other issues are display size and image quality. The display size of an image often has a misleading relationship to its file size. It's quite possible to display an image with a very large file size—one that could display with good quality at a size much larger than a computer screen can accommodate—in a relatively small display size. This effectively wastes most of the file size, bogging down page loading with no benefit to the user.

Tumblr and Copyright

Tumblr has an interesting relationship with the concept of copyright. Though the Web in general has been tough on copyright protection, with a great deal of protected content recopied for free, Tumblr users seem to feel particularly free to reuse others' content without attribution—except, in most cases, for a link back to the original source.

Reblogging seems to be seen as a kind of homage or gesture or respect—not as, well, stealing. Although there are exceptions to the copyright laws allowing for re-use as part of criticism and comment, it's hard to see how some of the reuse found on Tumblr would qualify. You may want to research the issue of copyright and the Web on your own, with reference to the specific kind(s) of content you would like to use.

It seems that standard practice on Tumblr, to a greater extent than on other blogging platforms, is to reblog freely. You can follow this practice without much chance of standing out, but be aware that your own original content that you put on Tumblr is likely to be freely reblogged as well. In fact, in Tumblr terms, this would be seen as something of a compliment!

Adding Your Own Photo to a Text Post

Tumblr allows you to do two things that are quite similar. You can upload a photo into a text post (text posts are described in the previous lesson), or you can upload a photo into a photo post, and then, optionally, add a caption to it.

If your post is image centered, using the photo post is probably easier. The caption, if you use one, has a well-defined relationship to the image. However, if the image is illustrating a text post, it's better to use the photo uploading capability in the text post.

The difference between the steps for uploading a photo from your hard disk and using a photo already on the Web are not intuitively obvious. Uploading a photo begins by clicking the Upload Photo link; using a photo from the Web begins by clicking a button that looks like a tree and is labeled Upload/Edit image.

CAUTION: If you upload a photo and want to embed it in text, text will not flow normally next to it unless you make a change in the HTML of your blog post. Follow these steps to make the necessary change.

Follow these steps to add a photo to a text post:

1. Prepare an image for use on the Web, as described in the previous section; resize and compress it appropriately. Store it in a place where you can easily find it.

2. From the Tumblr Dashboard, click the **Text** button.

   The Add a Text Post screen displays.

3. To upload a photo or other image from your computer, click **Upload Photo**.

   A window to help you find photos displays, as shown in Figure 7.3.

FIGURE 7.3   You can upload photos from your hard disk to Tumblr.

4. Find the photo you want to use on your hard disk, and click it. Then click **Open**.

   (The image should be prepared for web use, as described in the previous section.) The image displays in your blog post.

   Note that at this point, you can't resize the photo directly. If you know a bit of HTML, you can cause it to display in a different size by editing the HTML used to display it, as described in the previous lesson.

Text displays in the default position for web text, which allows only one line of post to display next to an image.

5. If you need more lines of text to display, click the HTML button. In the `<img>` link that displays, add these characters: `align="left"` for the photo to display to the left of flowing text, or `align="right"` for the opposite.

The result will look something like this:

`<img src="http://pixhost.com/110.jpg" align="left" />`

Adding a Web Photo to a Text Post

To add a web photo to a text post actually means adding a *link* to the photo; however, the photo displays in your post as if you had added it there.

> TIP: To put an image in your post with multiple lines of text flowing next to it, you must specify Left or Right as the alignment of the image, as described in the following steps.

Follow these steps to add a web photo to a text post:

1. Get the image URL.

Find an image on the Web that you like. Right-click the image, and choose Copy Image URL to copy the web address of the image.

If the choice Copy Image URL is not available, you can't find the URL from this instance of the image. Search the Web for another copy of the image that has a URL that you can copy in order to use it.

2. Get the image size.

Right-click the image and choose Properties, Inspect Element, or a similar option. The image's height and width will display, as shown in Figure 7.4.

FIGURE 7.4   The Tumblr logo is an image with height and width, too.

3. From the Tumblr Dashboard, click the **Text** button.

   The Add a Text Post screen displays.

4. To add a web photo to your post, click the **Insert/Edit Image** button.

   The Insert/edit image dialog displays, as shown previously in Figure 7.3.

5. Paste in the URL of the image that you identified in step 1.

   The Insert/edit image dialog displays.

6. If you want to add a description for the image, enter it under Image Description.

   The description displays as mouseover text and can be accessed by visually impaired users using a screen reader.

7. Specify the alignment of the image—usually Left or Right.

The choices are Baseline, Top, Middle, Bottom, Text Top, Text Bottom, Left, and Right. These choices relate the location of the image to nearby text; all the choices except Left and Right allow only one line of text to display next to the image, which is pretty useless in most cases. Left puts the image to the left, with multiple lines of text flowing next to it on the right; Right does the opposite. To further control the location of the image relative to text, you should edit the HTML directly, as described in Lesson 6, "Creating a Text Post."

8. If you want, specify the dimensions of the image, width first, and then height.

If you don't specify dimensions, the image displays full size. If you do specify dimensions, the image is resized to fit. If you enter dimensions that are smaller than the image and proportional to it, for instance, exactly half the height and width, it displays smaller, but otherwise normal. If you enter dimensions that are out of proportion, the image displays stretched in one dimension and compressed in another. If you enter dimensions that are in proportion but larger than the image, it might display pixelated or look otherwise unclear, as the image stretches to fit.

9. Click the **Insert** button to insert the image link into your post.

The description displays as mouseover text and can be accessed by visually impaired users using a screen reader.

Summary

In this lesson, you learned how to create digital photos for use with Tumblr and how to get the URL for web images for use with Tumblr. You then learned how to add either kind of photo to a Tumblr text post, flowing text around the photo if you want.

LESSON 8

Creating a Photo Post

In this lesson, you'll learn how to create a Tumblr photo post.

Photo Posts for Your Tumblog

In Lesson 7, "Adding Photos to a Text Post," I explained how to add photos to a text post, including how to flow text around a photo. This is one of two methods that Tumblr offers for posting photos.

The other is the photo post, which creates a post consisting entirely of one or more photos and, optionally, a caption. This approach highlights the photo(s) and keeps any words well out of the way.

Photo posts are best suited for worthwhile, interesting photos that stand out—photos that make their own point or that are well complemented by the caption underneath them. Photo posts are best suited for photos with a relatively large display size and fairly high quality; they should be at least a few hundred pixels in width, or more than half the width of a typical browser window. (Thinner photos just seem to beg to have text flowing next to them.)

> NOTE: As in the previous lesson, this lesson uses the word "photo" to also include graphics and other illustrations. For a brief overview of digital photo basics, see the previous lesson.

As I mentioned in Lesson 7, many tumblogs are just streams of re-blogged photos, original photos, or a mix. Use photo posts as the main approach in a photoblog or to liven up a more wordy tumblog.

Photo Post Options

Tumblr's Photo post button offers three ways to get a photo into your photo post:

- ▶ Upload a photo from your computer.

- ▶ Use the URL of a photo already on the Web.

- ▶ Take a picture with a camera attached to your phone, such as a webcam.

The first two options, using a photo already on your computer and using the URL of a photo already out on the Web, are also available for photos included in text posts; these are explained in Lesson 7. The third option, taking a picture with a webcam, is available only with photo posts and is explained in this lesson.

> TIP: Tumblr enables you to enter multiple photos, each with its own caption if desired, in a single photo post, but only for photos stored on your computer.

You can easily take a picture with your webcam and save it to your hard disk, then upload it, but the exact method depends on your webcam software. Using Tumblr to take the photo and put it straight into your blog post is simply a convenience, but it's a convenience that's available only for photo posts, not for text posts with added photos.

> CAUTION: Webcam pictures are usually low resolution and taken at an angle—and in lighting almost guaranteed to make you look bad. The photo angle is often at an angle that looks up the subject's nose, and the lighting is usually behind the subject, which is the worst place for lighting. Lighting should ideally be from behind the camera.
>
> Given these problems, the capability to import webcam photos into your tumblog posting directly or indirectly is a bit of a stupid pet trick. Kudos to you if you can take a good picture this way or otherwise find a worthwhile use for this capability.

Creating a Photo Post with a Stored Photo

These steps describe how to create a photo post using a photo stored on your computer. Later in this lesson, I describe how to create a photo post using a photo from the Web or one that you take at the time using a webcam.

Follow these steps to create a photo post using a stored photo:

1. Prepare an image for use on the Web, as described in Lesson 7.

2. From the Tumblr Dashboard, click the **Photo** button.

   The Upload a Photo screen displays, as shown in Figure 8.1.

FIGURE 8.1   Uploading a photo offers a lot of options.

3. Click **Browse**. Use the File Upload dialog box to find the photo, and then click **Open**.

   The path to the photo displays in the Browse area.

4. To see the uploaded photo without interfering with creating your post, click **Preview**.

A preview of the post showing the photo displays.

TIP: You might find that the photo is too big. You cannot resize the photograph or its display size in the photo post section of Tumblr. You have to use a photo editing program or website to create a smaller version of the photo if you need one.

5. Enter the caption (optional).

Note that the caption entry area allows only HTML entry. Use the buttons to insert the HTML tags for bold, italic, strikethrough text, or a link. To make specific text bold, italic, strikethrough, or link text, select the text, and then click the appropriate button. The text is surrounded by the beginning and ending HTML tags needed for the selected formatting. See Lesson 6, "Creating a Text Post," for more on HTML.

6. To give the user the ability to click on the photo to go to a different Web address, click Set a Click-Through Link (optional).

Setting a click-through link makes the photo act like a button in the sense that clicking it leads the user to a different web page.

When you click the link, an entry field opens up, titled Clicking This Photo Links to the URL. The entry field already has http:// in it.

7. To finish setting a click-through link, enter the URL of the destination in the entry field.

To copy and paste a link that already includes http://, paste over the same characters already present in the text entry box.

8. To preview the post, click the **Preview** button.

The post opens in a new tab. Return to the current tab to make any further changes and create the posting.

9. If you want to add another photo from your computer, click the button **Add Another Photo**. Repeat steps 3–8 for each photo you add in this way.

Another entry area opens, enabling you to add another photo, as shown in Figure 8.2.

FIGURE 8.2   You can upload multiple photos from your computer to a single photo post.

10. To create the post, click the **Create Post** button. To terminate the process without creating a post, click **Cancel**.

If you click Create Post, the post is created and displays on your tumblog.

Creating a Photo Post with a Web Photo

Creating a photo post with a photo available from the Web is similar to using a photo on your computer. However, you don't have the option of including multiple photos in a single photo post, as you do with photos stored on your computer.

Web Browsers Can Display Web Pages Quite Differently

To create a photo post with multiple photos using photos from the Web, find the photo on the Web, then right-click it and use the context menu that displays to save it to your hard disk. Follow the steps in the preceding section to use the saved photo in a multiple-photo posting. You can also use multiple photos from the Web in a text posting, as described in the previous lesson.

Follow these steps to create a photo post using a photo from the Web:

1. Find an image on the Web and copy its URL, as described in the Lesson 7.

2. From the Tumblr Dashboard, click the **Photo** button.

The Upload a Photo screen displays, as shown in Figure 8.1.

3. Click the link **Use a URL Instead**.

A text entry box titled Photo URL displays. The entry field already has http:// in it.

4. Enter the URL of the photo in the entry field that displays.

To copy and paste a link that already includes http://, paste over the same characters already present in the text entry box.

5. To see the uploaded photo without interfering with creating your post, click **Preview**.

6. Enter the caption (optional).

Note that the caption entry area allows only HTML. Use the buttons to insert the HTML tags for bold, italic, strikethrough text, or a link. To make specific text bold, italic, strikethrough, or to link text, select the text and then click the appropriate button. The text will be surrounded by the beginning and ending HTML tags needed for the selected formatting. See Lesson 6 for more on HTML.

7. Set a click-through link by clicking the link **Set a Click-Through Link** (optional).

As noted earlier, setting a click-through link makes the photo act like a button.

When you click the link, an entry field opens, titled Clicking This Photo Links to the URL. The entry field already has http:// in it.

8. To finish setting a click-through link, enter the URL of the destination in the entry field that opens.

To copy and paste a link that already includes http://, paste over the same characters already present in the text entry box.

Again, setting a click-through link makes the photo a button.

9. To preview the post, click the **Preview** button.

The post opens in a new tab. Return to the current tab to make any further changes and create the posting.

10. To create the post, click the button **Create Post**. To terminate the process without creating a post, click **Cancel**.

If you click Create Post, the post will be created and appear on your tumblog.

Creating a Photo Post with a Webcam Photo

Creating a photo post with a webcam photo is similar to using a photo from the Web. As with using a photo from the Web, you don't have the option of including multiple photos in a single photo post, as you do with photos stored on your computer.

To create a photo post with multiple photos using photos from your webcam, use the webcam's software to save photos to your hard disk first and then follow the earlier instructions for posting with multiples photos from your own computer.

Follow these steps to create a photo post using a photo from a webcam:

1. From the Tumblr Dashboard, click the **Photo** button.

The Upload a Photo screen displays, as shown in Figure 8.1.

2. Click the link **Take a Photo!**

A small dialog box called Adobe Flash Player Settings displays, as shown in Figure 8.3.

FIGURE 8.3   A tiny dialog box enables access to multiple settings for your webcam.

3. To change settings for your webcam, click any of the five buttons: Click **Display** to enable or disable hardware acceleration; click **Privacy** (the default) to allow or forbid Tumblr to access the image stream from your webcam; click **Local Storage** to allocate storage for Tumblr to use for this purpose; click **Microphone** to change microphone settings for video clips (more appropriate for a video post, as described in Lesson 13, "Posting Videos"); and click **Camera** to choose which camera to use, if you have more than one. Click **Advanced** to see an Adobe page describing these options in detail.

In most cases, you won't need to use these options, but you may want to do so out of interest or if you need to solve a problem that arises.

4. Click **Allow** to allow access to your camera.

A live stream from the webcam displays.

5. Click **Close** to get the window out of the way, and then click the **Snap Photo** button to snap the photo.

A countdown timer displays 3, 2, 1, and then the photo is taken.

6. To retake the photo, click the link **Retake Photo**. To see the settings dialog again, right-click anywhere on the image stream and choose **Settings** from the context menu that appears.

7. Repeat steps 5 and 6 until you're happy with the photo.

8. To use the photo as your avatar in Tumblr, select the **Make This My Avatar** check box.

9. Enter the caption (optional).

Note that the caption entry area allows only HTML. Use the buttons to insert the HTML tags for bold, italic, strikethrough text, or a link. To make specific text bold, italic, strikethrough, or link text, select the text and then click the appropriate button. The text is surrounded by the beginning and ending HTML tags needed for the selected formatting. See Lesson 6 for more on HTML.

10. Set a click-through link by clicking the **Set a Click-Through Link** (optional).

Setting a click-through link makes the photo into a button, in the sense that clicking it leads to a different web page.

When you click the link, an entry field opens up, titled Clicking This Photo Links to the URL. The entry field already has http:// in it.

11. To finish setting a click-through link, enter the URL of the destination in the entry field that displays.

To copy and paste a link that already includes http://, paste over the same characters already present in the text entry box.

Setting a click-through link makes the photo act like a button in that clicking it leads to a different web page.

12. To preview the post, click the **Preview** button.

The post opens in a new tab. Return to the current tab to make any further changes and create the posting.

13. To create the post, click the **Create Post** button. To terminate the process without creating a post, click Cancel.

If you click Create post, the post is created and displays on your tumblog.

Summary

In this lesson, you learned how to create a photo post for your tumblog using one or more stored photos, a web photo, or a webcam photo. You also learned how to create captions using the HTML-enabled editor.

LESSON 9

Creating a Quote Post

In this lesson, you'll learn how to create a Tumblr quote post.

Quote Posts for Your Tumblog

The variety of types of posts is one of the secrets of Tumblr. It's the only widely used blogging service that has such a variety of posts. Another secret of Tumblr is the ease of using the variety of post types. By making text, photos, quotes, links, chats, audio clips, and videos all available from the top of the Dashboard, each available "at the push of a button," Tumblr encourages you to use them all at least occasionally.

Using these different post types is part of what makes a tumblog special. The posts encourage you to use a variety of media types. Many blogging tools differentiate between technically different types, such as text, photos, audio, and video, whereas Tumblr adds types that are different in more subtle ways: quotes, links, and chats. This helps break up the tumblog, varying its flow.

In this lesson, I show you how to create a quote post, which is a post that highlights a quote. It's up to you to create interesting ones.

> TIP: The specific look of a quote post varies depending on the theme you're using. However, the quote is always formatted distinctively, and in a manner different from the source. The source is usually right-justified.

Rules for Quote Posts

Tumblr and users' tumblogs might seem at first to be an example of the famous quote from the movie *Fight Club*: "The first rule of Fight Club is—there are no rules!"

Strictly speaking, no strict rules exist for Tumblr posts. However, there are some good ideas, which you should consider treating as rules when you first start using Tumblr. Using the following ideas will help you get your tumblog off to a good start:

▶ **Use quotes**—Quote posts are a Tumblr-only media type and quotes are cool when used properly.

▶ **Go big**—Or go once in a while. Quotes are best used occasionally. In most cases, however, an all-quotes tumblog would stand, too. Figure 9.1 shows an (almost) all-quotes tumblog.

FIGURE 9.1   An all-quotes tumblog can be fun.

► **Be clever**—Try to avoid quotes that are too commonly used. The best quote posts catch your own mood at the time. As the author says in her all-quotes tumblog, Little Miss, "Every *quote* means something to me, which is why I *post* it in the first place :)."

► **Reuse is good**—Repost others' quote posts when they're particularly appropriate to your tumblog.

► **Fit the flow**—Some quotes will fit particularly well with the other quotes in your tumblog, and therefore belong in your tumblog more than they would somewhere else. For instance, if your blog covers the history of cinema, a literary quote might not be as pertinent as a famous movie line such as, "Frankly, Scarlett, I don't give a damn."

► **Break the mood**—Irony is popular on tumblogs. Look for the occasional quote that contradicts what's around it in an interesting way.

► **Use sources**—Providing a source with a quote is optional, but it's best to provide a source in most cases; the source completes the quote, and makes it easier for people to follow up if they want.

► **Think before you link**—Some quotes, with their sources, are complete in and of themselves; in other cases, the quote is easy to find online and follow up on. Provide a link if it's particularly useful, but not if it's superfluous.

► **Use quotes as bread crumbs**—Some quotes are interesting in and of themselves, and others are part of a web page or website that's interesting. Try to find intriguing tidbits that people can follow up on.

Creating a Quote Post

The mechanics of creating a quote post are fairly simple. Follow these steps:

1. Find an interesting quote and the source. If you want to provide a link to the quote, have the URL handy as well.

2. From the Tumblr Dashboard, click the **Quote** button.

The Add a Quote screen displays, as shown in Figure 9.2.

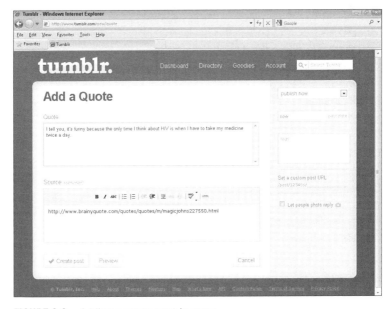

FIGURE 9.2   Adding a quote post is easy.

3. Type in or paste the quote into the Quote area.

Most quote posts don't use quote marks, because the formatting makes it clear that the words are a quote. (It's more obvious if there's a source than if there isn't.)

4. Optionally, add a source for the quote. Type the source in the Source area.

The source displays with different formatting under the quote. The Source area includes all the formatting capability of a text post, but it's generally not used, because a full text post would look odd in a quote post and with source formatting applied to it. The exception, where you should consider using formatting, is when linking from the source, as described in the next step.

5. Optionally, link to the source of the quote. Highlight the source text, or part of it, and click the link button. Enter the link URL, the title, and the target, as described in Lesson 6, "Creating a Text Post." (For details on link posts, see Lesson 10, "Creating a Link Post.")

The destination of the link for the source of the quote can be the original work from which the quote comes, biographical information about the person who said the quote, or other relevant resources. If you use a double-barreled source, such as "Magic Johnson quoted in the *LA Times*," each part of the source can have its own link. (In this example, you might link to a Wikipedia entry on Magic Johnson, and then to the article that contained the original quote in the *LA Times*.)

6. In the tags area, provide tags for the quote.

Tags are described in Lesson 6. Be sure to use tags that describe the quote but aren't in the quote or source. For instance, a Magic Johnson quote might be tagged "LA Lakers," "NBA," and "basketball," even if neither the quote nor source contains those words.

Magic is also famous for being a long-term survivor of HIV and for his business acumen. Tags relating to his HIV status, or tags relating to his business success, such as "billionaire," might be appropriate as well, depending on the quote.

7. Set the publishing date for the quote in the Publish date pulldown menu.

Summary

In this lesson, you learned how to create a quote post for your tumblog and how to make a quote post that works well in the Tumblr environment.

LESSON 10

Creating a Link Post

In this lesson, you'll learn how to create a Tumblr link post.

Link Posts for Your Tumblog

Link posts play a special role on Tumblr. A link post is a refined distillation of this special purpose of Tumblr. It's for sharing links to cool stuff you find online.

One of the best things Tumblr does is make it easy to share with others all the interesting things you find online. Tumblr also makes it easy to share cool things you find *offline*, such as photos.

Tumblr is a bit like *Star Trek*. Its users' mission is to explore the strange new world of the Web (as well as trying out what their new starship, Tumblr, can do). So, users share new stuff they find on the Web for examination and discussion.

Tumblr is often compared to and works particularly well with Twitter. Twitter, like Tumblr, is good for sharing interesting URLs. However, tweets just disappear into the ether. Tumblr postings accumulate in your tumblog. The accumulation of Tumblr postings says something about you, just as each individual posting does.

So, what should you use link posts for? Sharing everything you find interesting might work, but the best tumblogs seem to have a theme carved out from one or a few of their creators' interests. (For instance, the Garfield comic book, or a person's daily experiences in a big city.)

Your link posts can be to online resources that illuminate or explore your theme(s). For example, if you are interested in photography, you might link to other tumblogs that have a photography slant.

Link posts also allow a title—the default is the URL for the link, but that's rarely a good title—and a description. A good title is often a catchy phrase that relates to the link, such as the title, "I did it my way," for a link relating to classic male vocalists of Frank Sinatra's era.

You should use the description whenever the title is not self-explanatory, or when the link is a supporting resource and you want to use the description to make an argument. For instance, if you're linking to classic male vocalists, and the link title is "I did it my way," then a useful link description might be, "The work of classic male vocalists from the 50's through 70's—including Frank Sinatra, Mel Torme, and many others."

In addition to creating a link post directly, as described in this lesson, there are several Tumblr tools that are great for quickly creating link posts. See Lesson 18, "Extending Tumblr with Comments, Goodies, and Apps," for details.

> TIP: As with quote posts—described in the previous lesson—the specific look of a link post varies depending on the theme you're using. However, the link post is usually formatted distinctively, and in a manner different from a regular text post. See Figure 10.1 for an example.

Rules for Link Posts

You can do as you like with your link posts, but a look around Tumblr will give you an idea of some ways to use link posts that are more effective than others. Here are some ideas:

- ▶ **Use them**—As with all of Tumblr's post types, part of the charm of using Tumblr is to make good use of all of its posting types. Because they're so brief, link posts are meant to be light and spontaneous. If you use them properly, they will add life to your tumblog.

- ▶ **Consider an all-links tumblog**—A tumblog made up entirely (or nearly entirely) of link posts might be a good way to share part of your worldview with people. Figure 10.1 shows an example.

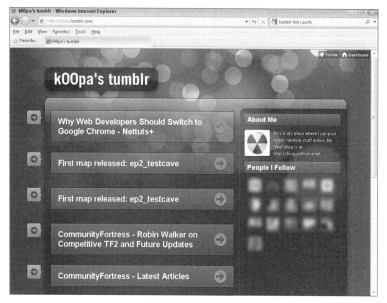

FIGURE 10.1   Links in tumblogs are interesting only if you make them that way.

▶ **Support your areas of focus**—Links to absolutely anything that interests you may seem random. Try to support the areas of focus shown by the other kinds of posts in your tumblog.

▶ **A link post is a homage**—If you're recommending that your Tumblr visitors leave your lovely tumblog for some other site, it should be a good one. When creating a link post, only the best will do.

▶ **Provide descriptions only when necessary**—Tumblr values brevity. You do not always need to provide descriptions. Using a link post instead of a standard text post to make a point can be an interesting change in your flow of posts, as can providing some link posts with descriptions, and some without them.

Creating a Link Post

If you've created posts of other types, creating a link post is easy. To do so, follow these steps:

1. Find an interesting link and have the URL handy.

2. From the Tumblr Dashboard, click the **Link** button.

   The Add a Link screen displays, as shown in Figure 10.2.

FIGURE 10.2   Adding a link post is simple using the Add a Link screen.

NOTE: When the user clicks on a link post's title, the link destination web page replaces your tumblog in the current browser window or browser tab. To avoid this, the user can right-click and open the link destination in a new browser window or browser tab.

3. Type in or paste the URL for the link in the Quotes area.

If you don't add a title, the URL will be used as the title.

4. Optionally, add a title. (This is recommended.)

The title displays in place of the URL. Clicking the title will lead to the URL. The current browser window contents—that is, your tumblog—will be replaced by the content at the link's destination. Unlike a link in a text or quote post, you can't change this.

5. Optionally, add a description.

The description for your link post has all the text-formatting capabilities of a text post, as described in Lesson 6, "Creating a Text Post."

If your link post title is self-explanatory, you do not need to add a description. However, it can be interesting to do so, and is especially valuable for variety if you use a lot of link posts.

6. In the tags area, provide tags for the link post.

Tags are described in Lesson 6. For posts with only a title and no description or no title, tags are particularly important because a search engine will have very little to go on otherwise.

When tagging any post, try to think like a user who's trying to come up with a good search term for your post: "Oh, that's the one about X." Figure out what X might be, and use the answers for tags.

7. Set the publishing date for the quote from the Publish date pull-down.

8. Create a custom post URL.

9. Click the **Preview** button to preview the post, or click the **Create Post** button to create it.

Summary

In this lesson, you learned how to create a link post for your tumblog and make link posts that work well in the Tumblr environment.

LESSON 11

Creating a Chat Post

In this lesson, you'll learn how to create a Tumblr chat post.

Chat Posts for Your Tumblog

Chat posts are pretty specialized, even for Tumblr, with its many kinds of posts, all equally available from the top level. A *chat post* is a post in which two or more people or characters exchange comments. Tumblr automatically formats the comments from the different "speakers" distinctively, so that it's visually easy to pick up who's "speaking" with a given comment.

I have a lot of respect for Tumblr and its support for a variety of ways of communicating, but chat posts, until you get used to using them, seem to border on being a stupid pet trick. However, if used correctly, even chat posts—which might be the least frequently used and the least obviously useful type of post on Tumblr—have their charm.

Chat posts are quite demanding to write because you aren't just blathering away about whatever you're thinking, as in most blog posts (and not just in Tumblr). You actually have to *write*. That is, you have to hold in mind two or more characters, real or imaginary, and have each "speak" in a distinctive voice.

For real conversations, this is a bit tough, because you have to remember what each person said well enough to convey not only the facts but the personality of each person in the conversation. For imaginary conversations, it's very tough, because you have to mentally switch between the participants' perspectives as you write. (Many professional or aspiring writers say that dialogue is the toughest thing to write. Perhaps that's why some modern movies, such as "action" films, tend to have so little of it!)

Even Tumblr bloggers, as cool as many of their tumblogs are, seem to hesitate to take on this challenge. Chat posts seem to be relatively little-used on Tumblr.

So, take up the challenge. Try to find a cool way to use a chat post occasionally. (For example, you might try a chat post to break up the tone of your blog, from talking "at" the reader to having the reader figure out the message from a dialogue between two other people.) Your tumblog visitors are likely to be glad you did.

> TIP: As with quote and link posts—described in the two previous lessons—the specific look of a chat post is different depending on the theme you're using. The "speech" of each "speaker" should be distinctive in the chat post.

Rules for Chat Posts

You have a lot of flexibility with chat posts. Even Tumblr users, who seem to make an effort with other types of posts, don't seem to use them very much. Here are some ideas:

- ▶ **Use them occasionally**—You'll be a good citizen of Tumblr if you manage to use chat posts occasionally, since many tumblogs never use them at all; you get extra credit for using them well.

- ▶ **Highlight interesting discussions**—Chat posts are great for creating a record of interesting conversations, in an easy-to-follow form. When you have an interesting discussion—live or online—use it as the basis for a chat post. (Be sure, though, that you have permission from the other parties who were involved in the exchange first.)

- ▶ **Use titles**—Titles are optional for chat posts, but they just beg for a witty description or ironic comment in the form of a title.

- ▶ **Follow up with other post types if needed**—There's no description field in chat posts, so you may want to follow your chat post with a text post that describes it or adds color. It might seem odd to use two different kinds of posts in this way, but hey, whatever gets the job done!

Unlike quote posts and link posts, I'm not recommending that you consider starting an all-chat posts tumblog. If you do, though, and you make it work, it will definitely stand out on Tumblr.

Creating a Chat Post

Creating a chat post is easy, although visualizing how it will look on your tumblog might take a bit of practice. It goes something like this:

She said: Give me all your money.
He: That's easy, I don't have any.
She: Then give me all your lottery tickets.
He: OK, here's an expired one.

In some themes, every other line of dialogue will be in one color, and the remaining lines will be in a different one. This is intended to highlight each speaker in a different color, and it works fine, as long as you keep to a strict alternation between two (and only two) speakers.

Follow these steps to create a chat post:

1. If you have any source material, such as an email exchange, have it handy for reference.

2. From the Tumblr Dashboard, click the Chat button.

   The Add a Chat Post screen displays, as shown in Figure 11.1.

3. Enter a title for your chat post (optional, but recommended).

   In some cases, it may be easier to come up with a good title after you write the post—perhaps even after you preview it.

4. Enter the dialogue for the chat post.

   The dialogue for your chat post has none of the text-formatting capabilities of a text post, unlike all the post types described in previous lessons.

FIGURE 11.1   Adding a chat post is simple.

You have only "he said/she said" formatting. Start each line in the post with the name or designation for a speaker, followed by a colon. After the colon, list what the speaker said.

Sadly, Tumblr themes are not "smart" enough to differentiate among more than two speakers. Even themes that assign different colors to alternating speakers won't give a third color to a third speaker; it keeps matching the same color to the same speaker. You only get one color per speaker if you have an unbroken alternation between two, and only two, speakers.

5. In the tags area, provide tags for the chat post.

   Tags are described in Lesson 6, "Creating a Text Post." Chat posts have plenty of words in them, so you need to use tags only for concepts not referred to by name in the dialogue.

6. Set the publishing date for the chat post from the Publish date pull-down.

7. Create a custom post URL.

8. Click the Preview button to preview the post.

9. If you haven't already, consider going back to the post and creating a title for it.

10. Click the Create Post button to create the post.

Summary

In this lesson, you learned how to create chat posts, a less-commonly used form of Tumblr post, and you learned how to create chat posts that work well in the Tumblr environment.

LESSON 12

Posting Audio Clips

In this lesson, you'll learn how to create or find audio clips and add them to your tumblog as audio posts.

Using Audio Clips in Tumblogs

Tumblr has a liberal policy on MP3 files. You can freely upload one MP3 file a day to Tumblr, up to 10MB in size, and Tumblr will host them for you. A typical three-minute song is about 3 minutes long, so 10MB is plenty for a typical song, but not for a 15-minute monster such as the famous In-A-Gadda-Da-Vida by 60's rock band Iron Butterfly. Many other sites either refuse to host audio files at all, limit uploads much more sharply, or charge for the privilege. With Tumblr, you can also easily link to MP3 files hosted elsewhere and have them display in your tumblog as if they were hosted on Tumblr.

Why are other sites more restrictive? Three potential issues exist with MP3 files: file size, viruses, and copyright. MP3 files tend to be large—about one megabyte per minute, on average. It costs money to store large files, and potentially much more money to pay for the bandwidth to send a popular file to perhaps millions of people who might download it. Except for the 10MB file size limit, Tumblr has no formal limits to protect itself on this front. (If the MP3 file on your tumblog gets a million downloads, you might hear from Tumblr, though.)

Viruses and copyright are related issues. Many popular MP3 files are protected by copyright, and really shouldn't be available at no charge on the Web at all. This makes these MP3 files valuable, so bad guys put viruses and malware—nasty software that's not exactly a virus, but bad enough—on web pages with MP3 files and in the MP3 files themselves. If you go looking for MP3 files, you're at least as likely to get an infection on your PC as you are to find a cool song to play, or to add to your tumblog.

Still, Tumblr takes the risk, which is small, because Tumbler no doubt has sophisticated virus protection programs. It neither prohibits you from doing anything risky, nor does it warn you. You're free to do as you like.

So enjoy yourself creating audio posts to your tumblog. But, as they used to say on the TV series *Hill Street Blues*—whose theme song became a popular piece of music—be careful out there.

> NOTE: Other audio file types exist besides MP3, but you can't upload these audio file types to Tumblr. If you link to a non-MP3 audio file, some, or many, of your tumblog visitors may not be able to play it back.

Tumblr and Audio Copyright

Audio files are, in theory, strongly protected by copyright. Even lyrics—yes, just the text of the words that are sung in a song—are well protected. Book authors have been sued successfully for including more than a snippet of lyrics from a copyrighted song in a book.

Yet Tumblr and other blogging sites, not to mention all sorts of sites on the Web, allow MP3 files of strongly protected songs, and entire sites full of nothing but song lyrics, to flourish. Egregious offenders, like Napster, have been shot down. But the files are out there, if you're willing to brave the risk of viruses and so on to get them.

However, it's best to avoid copying someone else's files, or even linking to them in a way that makes it look like they're on your site. Many people think it's tacky, or worse. Instead, if you think a song is interesting, provide a link to the page where the file is hosted. (You can do this from within several kinds of post, so you don't need the audio post for this.) That way, it's clear where the responsibility lies.

Digital Audio Basics for Tumblr

Sound waves are naturally analog—that is, continuous. Converting them to digital media files means that you have to sample the sound wave a number of times per second and convert the sound, at the time of sampling, into one or more numbers that describe the sound.

The more times per second that you sample, and the larger the number(s) that you use to describe each sample, the better the quality of sound will be. Unfortunately, at the same time, the larger the resulting file will be as well.

> NOTE: A sound sample is a representation of one moment of sound. Digital audio is created by taking thousands of samples per second and playing them back at the same speed, creating what sounds like continuous music or speech.

MP3 is short for MPEG Level III, a specific standard for creating and playing back sound files. The sound quality on MP3 files is not that great—it tends to drop highs and lows and to sound "cold," as distinct from the "warm" sound of, for instance, an old-fashioned record or a live performance. However, people have gotten so used to the sound of MP3 files that they often prefer it, in tests, to demonstrably better, higher-quality recordings.

The main advantage of MP3s is file size. You get about 1 minute of sound for 1MB of storage on MP3s. When the first iPod music player was introduced by Apple with a 1-inch, 10MB hard disk, this meant you could get thousands of songs on your iPod. Today, you can get much more storage on a similar volume of flash memory, which is more expensive than a hard disk but has no moving parts, and hard disks themselves are many times larger at a given size.

MP3s are also great for use on the Internet. Even on a fairly fast, 1Mbit/second connection, it takes about eight seconds to download a song. (That's because there are eight bits in a byte, and eight megabits in a megabyte.) On a slower connection, such as on your cell phone, it takes longer. No one wants to wait long for a song to play, so MP3 continues to be a good compromise for mobile and online music.

A lot of software tools exist for digitizing live or recorded audio and for editing and converting sound files. These tools, and techniques for using them, are outside of the scope of this book. You can find a lot of useful information online, and in books, if you want to learn more.

For the purposes of this lesson, we take for granted that you know how to get MP3s from the Internet or make your own, and that you understand the applicable laws where you live and aren't breaking them. In this lesson, we'll show you how to use MP3s in your tumblog.

Playback Support

Windows PCs differ in their support for audio file playback. A few older PCs even lack sound playback hardware, either because the manufacturer was cheap, or the original buyer—think corporate IT departments—didn't like it. Macs all come with Apple's QuickTime software, which plays back several audio file types, including MP3s. Macs also come with sound playback hardware, unless someone in your corporate IT department has removed it. If you link to a non-MP3 audio file, a visitor to your site who uses a Windows PC might not be able to play it back.

Why MP3s Are Great in Tumblogs

Despite its complexities, music files in general, and MP3s in particular, are wildly popular on the Web. So Tumblr, which enables people to share and comment on the best of the Web, has to support audio clips.

Audio clips add another dimension to tumblogs. Reading involves some parts of your brain; pictures get others going. (And, as the old saying goes, "a picture is worth a thousand words.") But audio files add an entirely new dimension.

Spoken words are more effective, in important ways, than written words. That's because hearing words spoken engages our emotions much differently than reading them, which basically requires us to speak them to ourselves. The speaker's (or singer's) tone of voice, inflection, phrasing, and other aspects affect how we hear what a person says.

Music, on its own or accompanying singing, affects us in other important ways. It conveys both emotion and meaning, although describing that meaning is famously difficult. People who watch a movie, for example, remember the background music vividly; to them, it isn't background at all. Others hardly notice it consciously, but are still affected by it.

Now tumblogs, and the Web in general, are great for many kinds of music files, but terrible at providing background music. Every time you surf to a different web page, you lose the old page as an audio source, and the new page may start playing its own audio. Even if you're surfing to different pages on the same website, each new page is a new beginning for audio.

This means there's no reliable way to get background music over the Web, except by downloading a file and playing it back on your PC or on a portable music player. (You can fake it, though, by keeping a page open that plays music, and not keeping open other pages that are playing music.) So think about this when you use audio in your tumblog. With all the hassles around audio, your user has to be fairly clever to get much out of it.

However, savvy users can appreciate good audio content. Tumblogs tend to be "cool" and ironic. A lot of music is cool and ironic. So you can use music to fit in with the prevailing mood of Tumblr—or go against it in interesting ways.

You can use audio to support the overall theme(s) of your tumblog, or to contrast against it in different ways. If you always write about peace and love, having an audio clip of thrash metal might reveal a whole new side of your personality! You can see lots of examples of music-related tumblogs at www.tumblr.com/directory/music.

Solving Problems with MP3s in Tumblogs

There are issues with MP3s in tumblogs, just as there are advantages. It's easy to sum up the main issues:

CAUTION: More than any other kind of file, MP3 audio files are associated with theft, viruses, nasty letters from Internet service providers, and so on. An entire company, Napster, became wildly popular and well known, and then was sued out of business, entirely based on its offering of free (but, mostly, copyright-protected) MP3 files for download.

Searching for MP3s online is risky. You can find yourself on web pages that are full of viruses and malware. Just visiting the site can give your PC a nasty infection. Actually downloading a file is even riskier.

A reference I found online to "the great trash heap known as MP3.com" is just one small example of this widely known problem. One web page I visited in researching this book wouldn't let me surf away from it; I had to close the browser window to move on.

▶ **Most people don't listen at all**—It's a bit of a hassle to play MP3s: Click, wait, hear, decide whether to keep listening, plus possibly turn speakers on or put on headphones and turn speaker or headphone volume up or down. Many people won't bother.

▶ **No one listens all the way through**—Web surfers are "twitchy" and have short attention spans. Few people listen all the way through an MP3 file, unless it's short.

▶ **Not safe for work issues**—Some MP3s are alarming or not topically safe for work; for instance, many songs contain obscenities. Warn people if the content or sound of an audio clip might be alarming or if a clip comes on loudly.

▶ **Mood impact is uncertain**—The best tumblogs have and maintain a mood, or even manage visitors' moods over time. Given that MP3s are a hassle, and that people listen to part of them or don't listen at all, how do you gauge their impact on your visitors' mood?

There are some good workarounds for these issues:

▶ **Do use audio clips**—Despite its hassles, audio adds a lot of liveliness to your tumblog. Music is a big part of life, offline and online. Engaging your blog visitors' eardrums, as well as their eyeballs, is a great way to add to your tumblog.

▶ **Include descriptions**—You should provide a description with your audio clip because more people will read the description before listening to the clip. This helps your site visitors judge the risk or reward of listening to the clip. Tumblr makes it easy, although optional, to include a description right alongside the clip.

▶ **Provide alternate sources**—If there's important information in an audio clip, such as someone reading a text, provide an

alternative source. For instance, if you use an audio clip of someone reading a text, provide the text, or a link to it. Audio clip
descriptions can be lengthy and can include links, so doing either
of these is easy.

▶ **Rely on experts and authorities**—A song from a hot new band
may seem attractive even to people who don't bother to listen to
it, because they recognize the title of the song or the name of the
performer(s); a reading by James Earl Jones is going to get more
listens than one by an unknown. (Except for a reading by you,
assuming you're unknown, because your tumblog visitors may
want to hear what you sound like.) The source of your clip may
be as important as the clip itself.

TIP: After you find an MP3 file, the process of getting the file or its
link is simple: Right-click the link to the file. (Unlike a photo, which
displays on your web page as an image, there's no visual represen-
tation of an MP3 file unless someone creates one.)

After you right-click the link, you'll get a context-sensitive menu with
a range of choices. The choices include Copy File Location, or similar wording, and Save File As, or similar wording.

To get the URL of a file, choose Copy File Location. The URL will be
put on the Windows Clipboard. Then go to any window you can use
for entering and editing text, such as a tumblog posting window,
and choose Paste (Ctrl+V). The URL is pasted into that location.

The URL may be quite complex, especially if the file is hosted in a
database. If so, don't worry—this is common practice. Here's an
example of such a URL:

http://www.amazon.com/MP3-Music-Download/b?ie=UTF8&node=
163856011

To test the URL, paste it into a browser's address bar and press
Return. The file should begin playing.

To get the file itself—and, unfortunately, any viruses that come with
it—choose Save File As. You'll be asked to navigate to a location
on your hard disk where you want the file saved. Go to the location,
click the Save button, and the file will be saved.

To test the URL, find the file on your hard disk and double-click it. It
should play.

Using MP3 Files in an Audio Post

You can use online audio clips in Tumblr in two ways. One is by reblogging someone else's audio posts. This is a well-respected practice in tumblogs, and leaves it clear who might be taking risks with copyright (not you).

The other way is by getting the URL to an MP3 file and including that URL in your audio post. Tumblr displays the file in your blog as if you had uploaded it yourself.

When such an MP3 clip is played by a visitor to your tumblog, it's actually transferred from the host's server to the user's computer. This does cause some cost to the host of the MP3 file. If the file is popular enough, it could cause substantial cost. This is more likely to be a problem for files that violate copyright than for files that don't.

Creating an Audio Post

After you've located a suitable file, creating a chat post is easy. Follow these steps:

1. Download the MP3 file you want or get its URL, as described earlier in this lesson.

2. From the Tumblr Dashboard, click tπhe **Audio** button.

   The Upload an Audio Post screen displays, as shown in Figure 12.1.

TIP: To check whether a file is under Tumblr's 10MB limit for MP3 files while you're browsing your files, right-click the file and choose Properties from the context-sensitive menu that displays. Check whether the file size is less than 10MB. If it's more, you'll need to use a different file or edit the file you want down to less than 10MB.

3. To upload an audio file, click **Browse**. Locate the audio file on your hard disk and click Open. Then go to step 6.

   The file uploads.

FIGURE 12.1 Audio posts are easy.

4. To use a file hosted on the Web, click the link **Use an Externally Hosted Audio File**.

A text entry area titled Audio File URL displays. A warning displays from Tumblr as well: "**MP3**s only. The file will be streamed from this URL, not hosted by Tumblr."

5. Enter the URL.

The URL is used to provide the audio file to the user.

6. Optionally, enter a description for your audio file. This is recommended. You can use all the capabilities of a text post, as described in Lesson 6, "Creating a Text Post."

If you don't enter a description, the user sees only an arrow and the words "Click to play." The user won't see the filename. A description gives the user a much better way to decide whether to click. Also, in a description, you can address any potential user concerns about copyright law, viruses, and so on.

7. In the tags area, provide tags for the chat post.

   Tags are described in Lesson 6. Search engines have no way to identify words used in an audio post, or words that people would commonly use to search for it with, unless you provide them.

8. Set the publishing date for the quote from the Publish date pull-down menu.

   Suppose you want to publish three MP3s on your tumblog in one day—to commemorate a birthday, for instance. You can work around Tumblr's one file per day upload limit by uploading files in the days before the event and setting the publish date to the same day.

9. Create a custom post URL, as described in Lesson 6.

10. If you haven't already, consider going back to the post and creating a description for it.

11. Click the **Create Post** button to create the post.

Summary

In this lesson, you learned how to create audio posts—an exciting, if still somewhat rare, use of Tumblr. You also learned some of the advantages and disadvantages of using audio files.

LESSON 13

Posting Videos

In this lesson, you'll learn how to create or find videos and add them to your tumblog as video posts.

Using Videos in Tumblogs

If Tumblr's policy on uploading audio files—one MP3 file, up to 10MB in size—is impressive, then its policy on uploading videos is spectacular. In partnership with the video file-hosting site Vimeo, which is "movie" spelled sideways, you can upload a total of 500MB of files per week. This is large enough for an hour-long video of reasonable quality. This can be all in one file or in as many individual files as you like.

This is in addition to your use of YouTube or other video-hosting sites. When your video is hosted on these sites (or even on video), you can embed the video in your tumblog. Basically, you include a link to video in your tumblog; the video displays on your page as if it were hosted on the same site. (YouTube, among others, puts its logo on videos it hosts, so the process isn't completely invisible to the user.)

Video files don't have problems with copyright and viruses to the same extent as MP3 files. Fewer copyright issues exist, because web video is so much lower in quality and/or shorter in playback length than a typical, DVD-type video file. Web video quality is usually also worse than standard, pre-HD television. The owners of the copyright are simply less likely to consider the lower-quality copy to be a violation.

For similar reasons, there are fewer viruses because, being of distinctly lower quality, the files are not as attractive to potential victims of a virus. Even with all its problems, though, web video is still quite attractive to users, just because video, by its nature, can be so darn interesting. So, you can use video freely in your tumblog, within the limitations of web video, which, lest you forget, are fairly severe.

> NOTE: Although several popular video file types exist, most videos you create with standard video-editing software are accepted by most online video hosts. The video file is then converted to the host's format on upload; it's usually also compressed fairly severely, making somewhat of a mockery of whatever care you took to create the file in the first place. Accomplished videographers know how to work around this to a certain extent, and you can learn some of their tricks with some study.

Creating Video Files

Much of the fun on Tumblr has to do with sharing media that's already out there, and this is certainly the easiest way to use video in your tumblog. However, you might want to create your own videos as well. Capturing video files can now be done with cell phones, digital cameras, and video cameras that cost as little as $100 or so. But how do you edit the resulting video?

Online video-editing tools are available, but they tend to be limited because of bandwidth constraints. Instead of looking for ingenious workarounds, consider purchasing a low-end video-editing software tool. Good tools such as Adobe Premiere Elements, the low-end version of the powerful Adobe Premiere video-editing program, are available as shareware, giving you limited use for free, and with a purchase price of well under $100.

And finally, a warning. Although it's tempting to want to edit video you find online—to create a mash-up of dogs on skateboards, or kids saying the darnedest things, or some other interesting result, the quality of most online video files is too low to bother with. If you decide to bother anyway, the new, edited file will be re-compressed on upload, making it even uglier. So, in most cases, you should use video online "as is"; for editing, start with video you capture yourself.

Digital Video Basics for Tumblr

Video is the cutting edge of Internet multimedia. Efforts are continuing to improve quality, reduce pauses, and increase resolution and sound quality. The goal is full-screen, interactive video, supporting video phone calls, interactive sports watching, video games with real video, and much more.

The Internet is in a transitional stage on the way to this destination. People are working to become better creators. Small fortunes are being made—and larger fortunes are being lost—in a scramble to figure out how to make video work online.

For Tumblr, video—like everything else on the Internet or, indeed, in real life—is an opportunity for sharing and (mostly ironic) commentary. Video clips are shared, commented on, reblogged, and much more. A few video blogs with original comments are appearing as well. The Animators section in the Tumblr Directory, at www.tumblr.com/directory/animators, has several examples.

The problem of storing video and the costs of transmitting it, which were once prohibitive for many, have largely been solved by services like YouTube and descendants such as Vimeo. These services accept video uploads, compress the file, and store and serve the video for free. (Paid memberships to video sites allow larger files, more files, higher quality, and other improvements.)

Most video clips are stored in one of a few high-compression file formats and played back using Flash, a technique made widely popular by YouTube. However, Flash doesn't work on the wildly popular Apple iPhone nor on the new Apple iPad, so some sites experiment with HTML5 and other non-Flash playback.

Even with all these advances, some problems with online video continue. Pauses in playback are common. As average bandwidth increases, video sites increase resolution and frame rates, so any slowdown in transmission speeds, or trying to play back video on less-reliable networks such as the cellular network, causes playback to be interrupted frequently. Still, the march forward of video won't be stopped.

In this lesson, we assume that you know the basics of finding and playing back online video files, and that you have a fast enough online connection to play back videos as well as most people do—which, much of the time, is not all that well.

Why Videos Are Good for Tumblogs

Video use on the Web keeps expanding. However, video is an engaging and, often, emotional medium. It doesn't necessarily fit the "vibe" of many tumblogs and other media that Tumblr supports.

On YouTube, videos of dogs on skateboards or people falling on ski slopes and water skis fit right in. The latest music video that millions of people are watching belongs there. Tumblr, though, is more low-key and "cool." When using video on Tumblr, if you want to fit in the Tumblr environment, you'll want to find video clips that are more intellectually interesting, such as college seminars, or that you can make interesting comments about.

When you find videos that fit, you can use them to liven up your tumblog quite a bit. Video makes a great contrast to all the other media types you can use.

Making Videos Work in Tumblogs

Like audio clips, videos are a change in pace for a blog that's mostly words and still images. Many people won't play the video at all or will play just a few seconds of it. People also worry about an inappropriate sequence if there are other people around at home or, even worse, at work. In one famous incident, a male banker was caught looking at pictures of nearly nude women in the background of a financial news broadcast; with video, it's even easier for surprises to pop up.

To make video work on your tumblog, start using it—or at least experimenting with it. "Hook" your site visitors by giving some key fact about the video, such as the involvement of someone they respect in making it or a tie-in to something else that's also interesting. Include captions that enhance the video or can be appreciated even without playing it. Give non-video users other ways to get any needed information, such as providing it in text form or providing a link to a text-based description. Figure 13.1 shows a book describing how to get the most out of video.

FIGURE 13.1   It seems like everyone is becoming a video producer.

Getting a Video Clip or Its URL

When you want to include a video in your tumblog, and the video is already online, you can download the video, get its URL, or get what's called *embed code* to use.

Unlike with an MP3 file, just the URL for the file isn't enough to help most video files play back correctly. You need some associated information. In an effort to make things simpler, YouTube and a few other sites have included the associated information in a URL. So when you use a video from a video-hosting site, take the information the site gives you, either a URL or embed code. Tumblr will use either.

Creating a Video Post

You can use two types of video posts in Tumblr. The easy one to create is using a video file that's already on the Web. Uploading a video of your own is more complicated—but, ultimately, quite effective.

Using Embedded Video Clips

To create a video post using a video that's already online, follow these steps:

1. Find a video that you like on a video site such as YouTube, Vimeo, or others.

   If there's a particularly interesting part of the video for your purposes, note, in your description of the video, at what point in the video it occurs. This makes it more likely people will watch the video—at least, the part you point them to.

2. Find the URL and/or embed code associated with the video, as described in the sidebar. If there's an option to customize the code, take advantage of it if needed. The specifics of how to do this will vary with the source which you're getting the video from.

   On YouTube, both a URL and an embed code are offered; in Vimeo, only embed code is offered. YouTube and Vimeo both have an option to customize features, such as the color of the playback window and the playback window size, which updates the embed code to reflect your changes. For an example, see Figure 13.2.

3. Copy the embed code or URL from the video site. (If you have a choice, as on YouTube, you can use either—but use the embed code if you've customized it.)

4. Switch to Tumblr. From the Tumblr Dashboard, click the **Video** button.

   The Add a Video screen displays, as shown in Figure 13.3.

5. In the Embed a Video tab, paste the embed code or URL.

FIGURE 13.2   YouTube gives you customization options for embedding.

FIGURE 13.3   You can use several options to add a video.

6. Optionally, enter a caption for your video file. This is recommended. You can use all the capabilities of a text post, as described in Lesson 6, "Creating a Text Post."

   If you don't enter a description, the user will see only a still image from the video with an arrow to click to play the video; not even the filename is shown. A description gives the user a much better way to decide whether to click, and possibly some guidance as to where in the video to look first.

7. In the tags area, provide tags for the chat post.

   Tags are described in Lesson 6. Chat posts have plenty of words in them, so you need to use tags only for concepts not referred to by name in the dialogue.

8. Set the publishing date for the quote from the Publish date pull-down.

9. Create a custom post URL, as described in Lesson 6.

10. If you haven't already, consider going back to the post and creating a caption for it.

11. Click the **Preview** button to see how the post looks. Return to the Add a Video area to make any changes.

12. Click the **Create Post** button to create the post.

Uploading a Video Clip

To upload your own video clip, Tumblr has created a partnership with Vimeo. Among other features, a free, basic Vimeo account offers the following:

▶ 500MB per week of upload space, which can include one or more videos, within the overall 500MB/week limit

▶ No bandwidth limits on video file downloads

▶ No time limits on video hosting

▶ A customizable video player

To create a video post using a video clip that you upload, follow these steps:

1. Create a video, or download a video file from the Web to your computer and edit it, if necessary.

2. From the Tumblr Dashboard, click the **Video** button. Click the **Upload a Video** tab.

   A message offering a link to Vimeo displays, as shown in Figure 13.4.

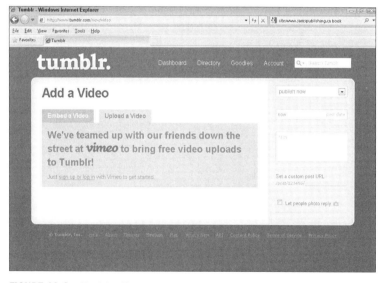

FIGURE 13.4   Tumblr offers a link to Vimeo.

3. Click the link to Vimeo.

   The Vimeo home page displays, as shown in Figure 13.5.

4. If you don't already have an account, use Facebook Connect to log in, or click the link **Join Vimeo**.

FIGURE 13.5 Vimeo is a newer video hosting service.

If you click the link Join Vimeo, the Vimeo home page displays, as shown in Figure 13.6. You're offered a choice of a Basic account or a Plus account. At this writing, a Basic account is free. A Plus account costs $59.95 as a one-time fee or $9.95 a month.

5. Create your account. Begin by entering your name, email address, and a password. Click the link Vimeo Terms of Service to read the ToS. Then click the check box **I Understand and Agree with Vimeo Terms of Service**. Click the **Join Vimeo** button.

You'll receive an email with a link back to Vimeo embedded in it. Click the link to complete registration. The Welcome screen shown in Figure 13.7 appears.

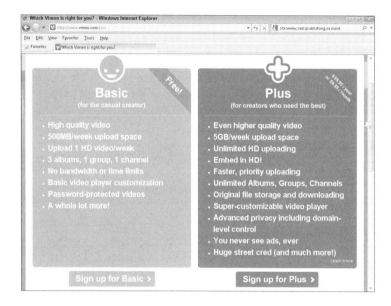

FIGURE 13.6 A Basic account will get you started.

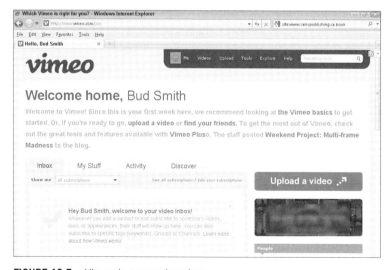

FIGURE 13.7 Vimeo is very welcoming.

6. Choose **Upload a Video**.

The Upload Your Video screen appears, as shown in Figure 13.8. If you have not yet created your video, or if you've captured it but not compressed or edited it, use the information on this page to help. You'll find recommended compression settings, a video tutorial, a help link, and more.

FIGURE 13.8   Uploading is easy—creativity is difficult!

7. Click the **Choose a File to Upload** button.

A File Open dialog box displays. Navigate to the video file and click **Open**. The video file uploads.

8. Embedding code is displayed alongside your video. Copy this code and use it in Tumblr.

TIP: If you're planning to host much video online, you may want to upgrade to a Vimeo Plus account. At this writing, it's a one-time cost of $59.95. For that, you get several features you might find worthwhile, as follows:

▶ No ad banners on your video clips.

▶ 5GB of storage per week or 1GB maximum per video. Instead of 500MB per week maximum, you get 500MB maximum per video.

▶ The video quality is better.

▶ You do not have to wait for videos to convert.

▶ You get unlimited High Definition video uploading, plus a free trial of 25,000 HD video plays. There no limit to uploading 1 HD video per week.

▶ You get complete player customization.

▶ You have unlimited groups, channels, and albums; basic users are limited to one group, one channel, and three albums.

▶ Privacy controls for who can use your videos, by domain name.

WARNING: Vimeo is for personal use only—and only for videos you create yourself (which should mean many fewer copyright issues than on other services). Business or commercial videos will be removed. There are specific video content restrictions, listed on the site, which you should follow. Vimeo also requests that comments about others' videos be positive in tone.

Summary

In this lesson, you learned how to create video posts in Tumblr and how to upload a video in Vimeo. You also learned some tips to get the most out of video files.

Liking, Reblogging, and Following Posts

In this lesson, you'll learn how to "like," reblog, and follow posts.

Building Community in Your Tumblog

Blogging is partly an attempt to build community around a topic or interest. Most bloggers feel gratified to know that a large number of people are reading their blog and to see comments or other responses to it, and to be quoted elsewhere. As a result, many bloggers are willing to invest time and energy to enhance the feeling of community around their blog by working to increase readership and to encourage commenting and other references to the blog.

Every blogging site has its own ways to build community, and Tumblr is no different. At least, it's no different in that you can build community. How it does so is actually a bit different.

Tumblr didn't start out allowing others to comment on tumblog posts. A couple of popular add-ins allow it, which I describe in Lesson 18, "Extending Tumblr with Comments, Goodies, and Apps." The Tumblr people are also experimenting with allowing comments directly, without an add-in.

However, even with add-ons and the possibility of Tumblr supporting comments, comments are not typically part of Tumblr's DNA. Instead, you respond to posts you like with one of three other methods, as follows:

▶ **"Liking" a post**—The first way to respond to a post is to "like" a post. This is confusing, because we all like some things and don't like others. But in Tumblr, to like a post means to click a little heart next to it. (It's like saying you "hearted" the post.) Your Tumblr login then displays a list of people who "liked" that post. This might inspire others who liked the post to visit your tumblog.

▶ **Reblogging a post**—In addition to "liking" a post, you can also reblog a post. This puts someone else's blog in your own tumblog. It's a strong form of approbation and can lead visitors to your blog to visit the tumblog you reblogged from.

▶ **Following a tumblog**—Finally, you can follow a tumblog. This is the strongest expression of approval; it's almost a kind of worship in social media terms. From the point where you follow a tumblog, every post from that tumblog displays in your own, including posts that are reblogged or followed themselves.

All these ways of encouraging others have a Tumblr-wide effect. Every tumblog is assigned a constantly updated rating called *Tumblarity*. The specifics of Tumblarity change with time and are kept secret, like the formula for Coca-Cola or the Colonel's recipe for Kentucky Fried Chicken. But having people like and reblog your posts, and follow your tumblog, are all potential contributors to a higher Tumblarity score.

The Tumblr-wide Directory is a list of top sites within Tumblr. The Directory is available as a link at the top of most pages in Tumblr. A high Tumblarity score gets your blog into the Directory, where it's quite likely to be noticed and attract lots more likes, reblogs, and follows.

Liking Tumblog Posts

The mechanics of liking a Tumblr post are simple. Just click the little heart next to a post if you like it. Several things happen as a result:

▶ Your user ID displays in a list of people who liked the post.

▶ Other people who liked the post—whether they liked it by clicking the heart or not—might visit your blog to see if they enjoy yours, too.

▶ Persons who created the posts you liked might visit your blog to see if they enjoy it, and they might like some of the posts you have included in your Tumblog.

People who visit your blog can also potentially see what you've liked and link to it. Whether your blog visitors see what you've liked depends on a setting in the Preferences area of your blog called Share Posts I've Liked. By default, this setting is set to Yes, but you can change it to No at anytime. To change the setting, visit your Dashboard and then go to **Account**, **Preferences**. When the screen shown in Figure 14.1 displays, change the setting.

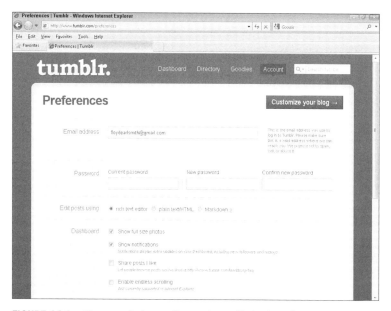

FIGURE 14.1   Share and share alike, or turn off sharing of posts you've "liked."

Liking posts is a form of commenting. However, because there's no actual comment, all that someone who sees the "like" can do to learn more it to visit your tumblog. They're then left to guess what the affinity is between the posts.

Liking a post adds to that post's Tumblarity ranking. If liking the post gets more visitors to your own tumblog, the visitors add to your Tumblarity ranking as well. Being predisposed to like your tumblog, they may like posts on your Tumblog, reblog your stuff, or even follow you, increasing your Tumblarity rating further. You may even get in the Directory.

Reblogging Tumblog Posts

Reblogging a post on someone else's tumblog puts that post in your tumblog. You have the opportunity to edit the post as part of reblogging it, but most tumbloggers do not edit posts. They reblog the original content as is. The point is to pay homage to the post by including it in your own tumblog.

Reblogging a post is potentially more work than liking it. However, it can also make your blog more interesting and, in a sense, more complete. That's if you do it right.

What's "doing it right"? The idea is that your blog has some kind of a theme. Perhaps the theme is obvious—something like "Japanese comic books of the 1960s." Perhaps the theme is simply "you"—your likes and dislikes. Then the idea is that *you* have a theme that shows some common thread connecting what you do and don't like. (The Brits put it this way: "What are you for?" Not in the sense of, "What are you in favor of?" but rather, "What use are you?") The visitor to your tumblog then has the puzzle, and the pleasure, of figuring out what that is. If they feel intrigued by that challenge, rather than put off by thinking that there's no real point to your tumblog, they may be more likely to keep visiting, and to like and reblog your posts, as well as to follow your tumblog.

So when you reblog, the idea is to make the repost your own—either by choosing posts to reblog that are perfect as is, fitting into and extending your theme, or by modifying the reblogged post, even slightly, to make it fit your tumblog better.

When you reblog a post, an editing window opens, depending on the type of post. The editing window enables you to change anything about the post that you want to change, and the changes you make don't show up as changes.

As you can imagine, this can be perceived as rude because your changes appear to be part of what you reblogged. So it's generally not something you should do. You should selectively pick posts in other tumblogs that work well in your tumblog without alteration or comment. (It's more acceptable to edit a post for length, removing things that are not on point for your own intent, than to actually change content into different content.)

A great example of this is the tumblog Garfield Minus Garfield, mentioned in Lesson 1, "Introduction to Tumblr." The tumblogger has carefully removed Garfield's image from each panel of that day's Garfield comic strip. Putting something in to replace Garfield would just look like vandalism. Taking him out, without replacing him, sometimes approaches art.

Here's an example of how to do reblogging:

1. Find a tumblog post you like.

2. Click the Reblog button on the tumblog.

The post displays in an editable window. An example is shown in Figure 14.2.

FIGURE 14.2 Reblogging lets you change everything, but it's usually best to leave reblogged posts intact.

3. Make any changes you want to make.

Refer to Lessons 6 through 14 for examples of what you can do with each type of post.

4. Click the **Preview** button to preview the post.

5. Click the **Reblog Post** button to reblog the post on your tumblog.

The post displays in your tumblog. An example of how this looks in one instance is shown in Figure 14.3.

FIGURE 14.3   Reblogging is a form of respect as well as an easy way to add to your tumblog.

NOTE: It seems logical that reblogging a post should help the host tumblog's Tumblarity more than liking a post and that liking should have greater effect than merely visiting. The details of just how much liking or reblogging might affect a blog's Tumblarity, however, are secret.

Following a Tumblog

To follow a tumblog is easy. Just click the **Follow** button. It changes to an Unfollow button, and shazzam, you're following the tumblog.

Following a tumblog is as favorable a comment as you can make about it. You are nonselectively and automatically importing all future postings to that blog into your own blog.

This is fairly common on Tumblr. However, it somewhat undermines the point of having a tumblog. All the wit, cleverness, and, yes, selectivity you apply to deciding what to put in your tumblog is set aside, except for the one initial selection, "I'm going to follow you." After that, you outsource your editorial judgment—which, to me, is what a tumblog is all about—to someone else.

Here are some suggestions for productive "following":

- ▶ **Choose terse tumblogs**—If you're going to republish someone, consider making it someone who posts rarely and well. If the person posts a lot, with only a few gems, reblog the good stuff rather than following the whole tumblog.

- ▶ **For a limited time only**—Consider following someone just long enough to get a few posts in; comment on them, and then drop the subscription. This is like an extended repost rather than an abdication of your tumblogging responsibilities.

- ▶ **Comment kindly, but incisively**—Ridiculing someone via their own blog posts is just mean. But using someone's posts as a springboard to your own insights and thoughts is great, perhaps the best use of following.

- ▶ **Draw connections**—Point out the connections between your interests and the tumblog(s) you're following. Let your tumblog visitors know why you're doing what you're doing.

- ▶ **Create an aggreblog**—Consider creating a separate tumblog that's a smart aggregation of several related tumblogs, perhaps with an occasional comment of your own. This is exercising editorial authority rather than abdicating it.

Following is a powerful way to help a tumblog's Tumblarity rating. There's no bigger thumbs-up you can give than following a tumblog.

The tag line for Twitter is: "What are you doing?" This has been criticized a lot, but notice the "you" at the center of it. If Tumblr were to have a similar tag line, it might be: "What are you thinking?" "You" is at the center of that, too. Your tumblog should reflect you; following people shouldn't get in the way of that.

Improving Your Tumblarity

The Tumblr community is, in some ways, quite close. You can certainly join Tumblr, start your tumblog, not communicate much with others, and live your own life. But many Tumblr users reach out to each other, either within an interest group or right across the service. Many people enjoy their interactions in Tumblr very much.

So the launch of Tumblarity caused a certain amount of angst. Tumblarity is a rating for your tumblog. It's made up of several elements:

- ▶ How many page views your tumblog gets.

- ▶ How many likes your posts get.

- ▶ How many reblogs your posts get.

- ▶ How many followers your tumblog gets.

- ▶ Secret factors, which might include how often you post and your use of a variety of media types.

Your Tumblarity rating is shown on your Activity page. It drives which tumblogs get included in Tumblr's Directory.

Tumblr users' comments are mostly that they don't like Tumblarity, or even that they hate it. There are two main types of complaints, as follows:

1. Seeing a low Tumblarity rating for one's tumblog is disappointing.

2. In pursuit of higher Tumblarity ratings, people's tumblogs change to include only stuff that might be popular, get a lot of search engine hits, page views, likes, reblogs, and followers.

The first problem isn't necessarily a bad one. People who truly find their low rating depressing might improve their blog to fix it, making tumblogs better, the service more interesting, and Tumblr more popular.

The second problem is worse, though. The "soul" of Tumblr might be lost in a mad dash by leading tumbloggers to get more traffic and activity, ultimately making the service *less* interesting and attractive.

At the time of this writing, the Activity page has been taken away while Tumblr figures out what to do with it. Even after initial decisions are made, it might change again. Visit the Activity page, see how high your Tumblarity rating is for your blog, and decide what, if anything, you want to do about it.

Summary

In this lesson, you learned how to "like" and reblog other people's posts, and how to follow their tumblog. You also learned what Tumblarity is and why it might—or might not—be important.

Posting by Email, Phone, and Audio

In this lesson, you'll learn how to post to your tumblog by email, text, or phone call.

Posting by Email and Phone

Much of what makes Tumblr interesting, unique, and fun is its status as a web service, run on the computer. With its built-in support for multiple types of data, Tumblr is a great match for just about anything you can do today on a computer.

The idea of sharing things you find online, commenting on all sorts of news and other people's commentary, and visiting, "liking," reblogging, and following other blogs and their posts, all make Tumblr a home for the various thoughts and impressions—important or unimportant—that you experience online.

However, Tumblr is too important to its millions of users to be left to only computer-based use. Tumblr supports posting by email and use from smartphones. Like the smartphone apps, the email posts are largely for phone use, because if you're on your computer using email, you might as well just post from within Tumblr. The advantage of email posting over using an app is that it's quick, reliable, and works from many more phones.

Cell phone use extends Tumblr in very interesting ways. Cell phones are with people all the time, so Tumblr, used from a cell phone, can reflect much more of your life. As more and more phones have cameras, video capability, and more, the range of media types that can be sent via a cell phone post is expanding to match what you can do on a PC.

Audio postings may even increase because of phone use. Google Voice, a new service for phone calling, automatically records voicemail messages and can be used to record conversations as well. Many of these might make good posts; some of my voicemail messages, for instance, have been pretty funny, even if often unintentionally so.

Sending Posts by Email

Tumblr has a great facility for posting by email, and it supports all types of Tumblr posts. You really should try it, and use it regularly. Tumblr calls it "incredibly sophisticated," and that's not far wrong.

To send a Tumblr post via email—from your cell phone or anytime email is more convenient to access than Tumblr is—follow these steps:

1. In Tumblr, click **Goodies**.

The Goodies page appears, as shown in Figure 15.1.

FIGURE 15.1   Tumblr offers lots of cool Goodies.

2. Copy the email address shown.

This is your secret email address for posting to your blog, and only your blog. If other people get access to it, they can post to your blog as well. This may, at the least, cause a slippage of your blog's editorial standards below your own normally high level, and at worst cause great embarrassment as someone claiming to be you posts to your tumblog.

3. If you're concerned at any point about the address having become known to others, click the **Reset This Address** link. You'll be given a new email address.

4. To test the email address, send an email message to it. Check that the message does indeed appear as a post in your tumblog.

That's it! You can now post to Tumblr at any time by sending an email to the address.

> CAUTION: Tumblr's capability to turn emails into different kinds of postings to your tumblog is pretty cool. But what happens if you send a posting to Tumblr via email, and you use a format slightly different from what's described in the following list? The result is—to use a word much beloved by computer programmers every-where—undefined. So, follow the prescribed format exactly, and when in doubt, keep it simple.

Tumblr doesn't stop there, though. It automatically assigns your email message to the appropriate type of Tumblr posting, depending on what you include in the email.

Here's how it works for different media types. You can even include tags if you want:

▶ **Text**—A typical text email shows up as a text post. If there's a subject line, it's used as the title of the post (optional).

▶ **Tags**—Add tags to a text post, or to any of the post types. Simply put the tags at the end of the post, with a hash mark and a space before each tag.

▶ **Photo**—An email with nothing but a photo in it becomes a photo post. If there's a subject line, it's used as a caption (optional).

▶ **Photo sets**—An email with nothing but several photos in it becomes a photo set post. If there's a subject line, it's used as a caption (optional).

▶ **Links**—An email with nothing but a Web URL in it becomes a link post. If there's a subject line, it's used as a description (optional).

▶ **Quote post**—An email with nothing but text surrounded by quotes becomes a quote post. If you follow the close quote mark with one or more spaces, a dash, a space, and words, those words are used as the source of the quote (optional). See the next section for information on how to link to the source of the quote using Markdown. See Figure 15.2 for an example.

FIGURE 15.2   Quotes become quote posts—with a source, if you'd like.

▶ **Chat post**—A text email with nothing in it but dialogue becomes a chat post. Each comment must begin with a speaker's name or designation, a colon, and the text of the comment.

> TIP: Create a contact in your contact database for your tumblog. List your secret Tumblr email posting address as the email address for your tumblog. And list the toll-free number for audio posts as the phone number. Then perform whatever steps are necessary to propagate the contact across your computer and cell phone. This will make it easy to find the email address and phone number when you need them, and to update if you generate a new email address to use with Tumblr.

▶ **Audio**—An email with nothing but an MP3 file in it becomes an audio post. If there's a subject line, it's used as a caption (optional).

> WARNING: When you post to Tumblr via email, there's no delay in publishing, no ability to preview a post, and no ability to quickly and easily look in your tumblog just after to see how it turned out (and then to delete it if you don't like the result).
>
> In an email posting, it's much easier to commit typos (which are a bit sniffed at on Tumblr, more so than on Twitter), to say silly things, and generally to fall below the standard of ever so slightly refined elegance that distinguishes the best tumblogs.
>
> Posting via email instead of from Tumblr's web interface is a bit like the difference between a chicken that lays eggs, and an egg. When you make an omelette, the chicken is involved; the egg is committed. When you create a post by email, you get committed much quicker.

Markdown and Email Posting

Markdown is an HTML alternative that's being evangelized by John Gruber, the force behind the well-known Daring Fireball tech blog. Markdown doesn't add any new capabilities; it's just a different, text-friendly way of entering many of the markup codes that distinguish HTML.

If you don't already know Markdown, you don't need to learn it for posting to your tumblog from your computer; it's easier to use the WYSIWYG editor or, if you must, HTML (because it's supported directly in the text-entry windows). Markdown is just another option.

Markdown, though, is quite convenient for posting by email. When you put formatting into an email that's sent to your secret Tumblr email address, Tumblr ignores any formatting. You need to use HTML tags or Markdown if you want to format the text in your posts or add links. Markdown is easier to remember—unless you already know HTML, in which case that's easier—and far easier to type.

Here are a few examples of Markdown you can use in your posts, plus one important "must":

▶ **Enabling markdown**—To put markdown into effect, include the following code: **!m**. This signals Tumblr to recognize markdown code in the message. Tumblr will remove the code from the message.

▶ **Bold and italic**—To make text italic, surround it with *single asterisks* (the asterisk character, like a star, not the word "asterisk"). To make text *bold*, surround it with **double asterisks**. (Goofy, I know.)

▶ **Links**—Links are one of the less-obvious formatting categories for Markdown. Surround the words you want to use as a link with [square brackets]; surround the link URL with (parentheses).

▶ **Lists**—Precede each item in an unordered (bulleted) list with an asterisk. Precede each item in an ordered (numbered) list with a digit and a period. (Markdown will ignore the actual numbers you use and replace them with 1., 2., 3., and so on.)

▶ **Special characters**—Markdown automatically replaces special characters, such as &, with their HTML equivalents, saving you a lot of hassle.

If you don't know Markdown at all, or don't know a specific Markdown tag that you need, or no Markdown tag exists for what you need, you can use HTML tags instead. They work interchangeably.

For more on Markdown, visit the Markdown page on the Daring Fireball blog at daringfireball.net/markdown. Consider creating a cheat sheet for yourself of commonly used markup characters.

Markdown is a good choice for simple HTML-style formatting in your emailed blog posts. Figure 15.3 shows an example of Markdown-marked text and the resulting display at a site called Markdownr, which you can visit at http://markdownr.com. The Markdownr site lets you enter Markdown-formatted text on the left and shows the result on the right. It also has a link for converting Markdown to HTML.

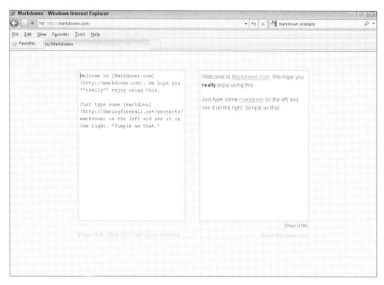

FIGURE 15.3   Use Markdown to mark up your emailed posts.

Posting via App

A service as popular as Tumblr is bound to get support for posting from various mobile phones. Indeed, in addition to email posting support, you can use a variety of ways to access Tumblr from your mobile phone. Here's a quick comparison:

Email posting—An excellent way to post, and it works from any cell phone that can send email, which, these days, means almost any cell phone. Email posting gives the broadest reach for at least some kind of Tumblr access.

Web access—Any cell phone with web access can access Tumblr and your tumblog. However, Tumblr is strongly dependent on screen size, and many tumblogs are quite data intensive, with high-resolution photos and so on. So the quality of your experience as a Tumblr user via cell phone will depend strongly on the screen resolution of your cell phone and how fast your Internet connection is. If the answers are "small" and "slow," don't expect to be able to do much.

Official apps—Tumblr has one cell phone app, for iPhone, which is reputed to be very good. Its main purpose is for posting to Tumblr via all its supported media types, including video. The app is available through the iPhone's App Store. Screenshots are shown in Figure 15.4.

FIGURE 15.4 The official Tumblr iPhone app makes good use of the iPhone's capabilities.

Tumblr also has an application programming interface that allows third parties to create applications of many kinds, including smartphone apps. Additional iPhone apps are available from third parties, as well as Android apps. There's also increasing support for Tumblr in Twitter clients on various platforms, although this is still evolving. See Lesson 18, "Extending

Tumblr with Comments, Goodies, and Apps," for more information about third-party iPhone apps, as well as the iPhone apps.

Posting via Audio

Tumblr supports creating audio posts by phone and gives you a toll-free number to call into. Audio posts are described in detail in Lesson 12, "Posting Audio Clips."

The Tumblr API

Creating an application programming interface, or API, for a web service is very important—and quite difficult. An API is a set of tools that are provided to external developers. It allows them to exchange data with, and request services from, the host service.

Creating and supporting an API is a sign of maturity for a technology company. To do so requires that the code running the company's services be documented, reorganized, and revised—often even rewritten—to be more reliable.

All this has to be done while meeting—or trying to fend off—user demands for further improvements in the company's offerings. Faced with this dilemma, some companies have delayed releasing a needed API for years, and some have even gone out of business under the strain of the efforts required.

Tumblr's accomplishment in quickly releasing an API for its relatively complex service, and successfully evangelizing developers to create applications using it, is notable. Tumblr has gotten good marks for improvements since the initial API release and has also added a Twitter-compatible version of its API. All this increases Tumblr's staying power, and the odds that Tumblr will continue to grow in the face of the intense competition now taking place among blogging tools.

This is pretty cool, but it's not a complete substitute for other kinds of posting. Here are the main reasons:

▶ **Not everyone listens**—As described in Lesson 12, not everyone listens to audio posts. In fact, most people who visit a given tumblog probably don't. Also, with this tool, you have no way to add any text at all around the audio post to alert the people who would be most likely to be interested that this post is worth their time.

▶ **Not editable**—You have no way to add text around the post nor to edit the audio. Unless you have a good radio voice and practice in public speaking, you're likely to sound unclear and uncertain, and perhaps have quite a few "uh"s in there as well.

▶ **There's a limit**—Here's another reason to speak well: Phoned-in audio posts are limited to two minutes in length.

However, in a pinch, audio posts, even the limited type you can create by calling in, are both fun and better than nothing. They're definitely worth using a couple of times for variety in your tumblog, and so that you're ready to use them when needed.

Audio posts are also useful for specialized purposes. If there's a cool song being played on the radio that you want to remind yourself of later, if you want to share the experience of a music concert, or if you just want to leave a (nonprivate) voice note to yourself, this is the way to do it.

Follow these steps to set up audio posts:

1. In Tumblr, click **Goodies**. Then scroll down to the bottom of the page.

You'll see the Call in Audio area in the Goodies page, as shown in Figure 15.5.

2. Enable Caller ID, if needed.

Tumblr needs Caller ID to recognize the phone call as yours and put the audio post in your blog.

3. Enter your phone number. If you're outside the United States and Canada, use all the digits someone would use to call you from the United States.

This will allow Tumblr to recognize the call when it comes.

4. Enter a PIN from one to four digits (optional).

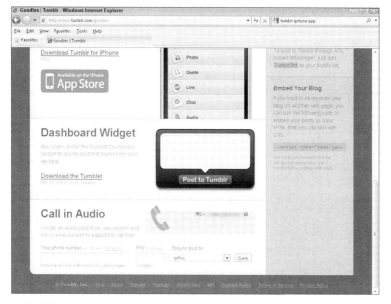

FIGURE 15.5   Set up Call in Audio so it's ready when you need it.

You can enter a PIN that you'll be required to enter when you call in your audio post, if you're really worried that someone will call into Tumblr from your designated phone number when you're not looking and try to blog in your name.

5. From the pull-down menu, select which of your tumblogs to post to, if you have more than one tumblog on your account.

6. Click **Save**.

    After you've done this, recording the post is simple. Call the toll-free number, 1-866-584-6757. Enter your PIN, if needed, and then you'll be prompted to record your message. Record your message and hang up.

Summary

In this lesson, you learned how to post to your tumblog by email, and you learned how to use HTML or Markdown for marking up your post. You also learned about the official iPhone Tumblr app and about the additional third-party apps available for iPhone, Android, and perhaps in the future for other platforms as well. Finally, you learned about creating audio posts by phone.

LESSON 16

Using Tumblr with Twitter

In this lesson, you'll learn how to flexibly combine two of the best services around: Tumblr and Twitter.

Using Tumblr with Twitter

Twitter has captured people's imaginations like few Internet services before or since. The idea of sending a stream of updates, 140 characters at a time, is a bit silly—yet quite powerful. Many people are active Twitter users, and many more follow various Twitter streams and send an occasional tweet of their own. Twitter even makes the news on a regular basis, and several books have been based on tweets.

Yet Twitter also suffers from some problems. Tweets certainly lack permanence. They also fail to build up into a more interesting picture, unless someone follows a person's tweets very closely and remembers them all. And the lack of support for anything except text and links is ultimately limiting in expressing yourself.

These are reasons why Tumblr works so well with Twitter. Tumblr can serve as a collecting point for tweets. Your tumblog can be entirely "powered by" tweets, in which case it just serves as a record and assembly point—not a bad use of Tumblr. However, you can also weave together a tumblog from tweets, emails (as described in Lesson 15, "Posting by Email, Phone, and Audio"), captured pieces from around the Web, and entries created directly in Tumblr. This way, your tumblog is fascinating not only for its entries, but for how they got there. The medium is the message, indeed!

But wait, there's more. The people who run Tumblr have not only made it a great destination for your tweets; you can follow your Twitter feed and respond to and send tweets within Tumblr as well. This is a convenience— a way of keeping an eye on Twitter while you're tumbling (or, if you prefer, tumblogging); it's also a way for what's happening in one service to inspire what you're doing in the other.

Finally, you can send your tumblog posts to twitter. Tumblr even lets you edit the post before sending. This is fine for people who do a lot of short text posts in Tumblr, but others will find that most of what's interesting in their tumblog entries gets lost in the translation to tweets. So, sending your Tumblr posts to Twitter may not work as well for most people, most of the time, as a Twitter-first approach.

Sending Your Tweets to Your Tumblog

If you tweet at all—whether a little or a lot—it makes great sense to send your tweets to your tumblog. This works well no matter which service you use more:

- ▶ If you're mainly a twitterer, a tumblog is a great long-term home for your tweets. You and others can get a good sense of what you've done with Twitter over time, you can pick up on old discussions, and so on.

- ▶ If you're mainly into Tumblr, your own tweets are just another media type for your tumblog. Your tweet stream is also a source of ideas and inspiration for your tumblog.

- ▶ If you value both, great opportunities exist for cross-fertilization, making for a very rich online experience.

Tumblr treats your tweets as a feed, like an RSS feed. Tumblr also accepts many other kinds of feeds:

- ▶ **General website updates and news**—RSS (which is supported by many kinds of sites).

- ▸ **Blogs**—Blogger, LiveJournal, Vox, WordPress.

- ▸ **"I like this" sites**—Del.icio.us, Digg.

- ▸ **Video sites**—Vimeo, YouTube.

Don't give up if the site you want to use isn't listed; updates to most sites can be used as an RSS feed. See the next lesson for details on using these other kinds of feeds. Tumblr can support up to five feeds per account, and your tweets will count as one of the five.

> TIP: If your updates are protected in your Twitter settings, no feed is created, so Tumblr can't import it. If you want to create a feed from Twitter to Tumblr, first go to Twitter.com and make sure your updates aren't protected.

Follow these steps to send your tweets to your tumblog:

1. In Tumblr, choose **Account**, **Preferences**.

   The Preferences page appears.

2. Click the **Customize Your Blog** button.

   The Customize page appears.

3. Click the **Services** menu.

   The Services menu drops down.

4. In the area labeled with an RSS button and the words Automatically Import My, choose Twitter from the pull-down menu.

5. Enter your Twitter username in the text entry area.

6. Click the **Start Importing This Feed** button.

   A message appears, showing that your feed is being imported, as shown in Figure 16.1. All your feeds are shown in this way.

   Twitter feeds are imported as full text without titles. Because there's no title in Twitter, there's nothing for Tumblr to import as a title.

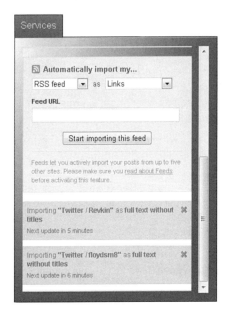

FIGURE 16.1   Feed your tumblog with your tweets.

7. Click the **Save + Close** button to save the changes and return to the Preferences page.

Your most recent tweet is imported, if it was made within the last two days. Tweets from this point forward are imported as well.

Fresh tweets are updated about once an hour. (This is not very fast for a Twitter user, who typically wants everything up to the second, but that's the breaks.)

> WARNING: If you don't log into Tumblr or post directly to Tumblr fairly regularly, feed imports such as your Twitter feed will become inactive. Note that Tumblr leaves the meaning of the words "fairly regularly" undefined, which gives them leeway to be flexible, or to crack down if too many people use Tumblr only as a sort of final resting place for tweets.

Posting and Viewing Twitter in Tumblr

You can view your Twitter feed within Tumblr and post tweets as well. This is becoming a more frequent offering within not only Tumblr but other web-based services, such as sites that allow you to watch video.

As far as I can tell, there are two purposes: The first is that you can use Twitter to comment on what you're doing (on Tumblr) or watching (on a video site). The other is that many Twitter users are so obsessed with Twitter that they have to be able to view their Twitter feed within other services. Otherwise, the user will be distracted, and quickly pulled away, by Tumblr.com, TweetDeck, or tweets arriving on their smartphones.

> TIP: Sending your tweets directly to your tumblog, as described earlier in this lesson, can certainly be worthwhile. However, you can also have all your tweets go into your Dashboard, and choose which of them to reblog from there.

Follow these steps to view your Twitter feed, and post to Twitter, from within your Tumblr Dashboard:

1. In Tumblr, choose **Account**, **Preferences**.

   The Preferences page appears.

2. Scroll down to the Twitter area.

   The Twitter area, and other areas of your Preferences page, appear, as shown in Figure 16.2.

3. Enter your Twitter username and password.

   Click to set the check box to show Twitter updates in your main Dashboard feed, or clear the check box to not show them. Note that Tumblr recommends showing the Twitter updates only if you're following a small number of Twitter users and, most likely, ones who don't tweet constantly.

FIGURE 16.2   Set preferences for tweeting into your tumblog.

You'll see a link, **Disable**, appear after you enter your Twitter username and password. Clicking this link clears your username and password and stops the live Twitter connection within Tumblr.

To stop tweets from showing up in your Dashboard, while keeping your Twitter username and password in place, clear the **Show Twitter Updates** check box in your main Dashboard feed.

4. Click **Save Preferences**.

Your Twitter connection will start. Figure 16.3 shows how it looks with Twitter updates in your main Dashboard feed.

After you have tweets coming into your Dashboard, you can do the following:

▶ Reblog a tweet into your tumblog by clicking the **Reblog** button.

FIGURE 16.3   Tumblr can certainly overwhelm your Dashboard.

▶ Reply to the tweet from within your Dashboard by clicking the **Reply** button, which is a curvy arrow.

▶ Mark the tweet as a Favorite by clicking the **Star** button.

Quality Versus Quantity

Tumblr's recommendation that you follow only a few people if you're going to include tweets in your Dashboard highlights an interesting difference in the services. Tweets in your Tumblr Dashboard are no more overwhelming than they are anywhere else. So why the recommendation from Tumblr?

It seems to me that Twitter has a "full immersion" approach. You get a ton of tweets, most of which might not be all that interesting or useful (something you'll be reminded of if you carefully go through all the tweets you receive, deciding which ones are worth reblogging into Tumblr). It's up to you to separate the wheat from the chaff.

Tumblr has a much more selective approach. Tumblr postings are meant to be, for want of a better word, elegant. They should be carefully chosen, specifically highlighting some aspect of you or your mood.

To make the best use of Twitter in Tumblr, you might consider following fewer people, which somewhat undermines the point of Twitter, at least as it's generally used, but might also get you some of your precious time back.

TIP: You'll have noticed that tumblogs take advantage of the full width of even a widescreen, such as a typical laptop with its 1280x800 resolution. So squeezing Twitter in there, too, may not be to your liking. You might be better off taking Twitter out of your Tumblr account and switching back and forth between Tumblr and a Twitter client, such as Tweetdeck.

Most laptops have a connector and enough video memory support to allow you to plug in a second monitor. With Tumblr on one screen and Twitter on the other, you may be a very happy camper indeed.

Sending Tumblr Posts to Twitter

Sending Tumblr posts to Twitter is generally a good thing. You can choose whether to send a specific post on a post-by-post basis. This allows you to tweet only those Tumblr posts that make sense as tweets.

The steps to send your Tumblr posts to Twitter are very similar to getting Twitter as a feed, as described earlier in this lesson.

Follow these steps to give yourself the option to send each of your tumblog postings to Twitter:

1. In Tumblr, choose **Account**, **Preferences**.

    The Preferences page appears.

2. Click the **Customize Your Blog** button.

    The Customize page appears.

3. Click the **Services** menu.

    The Services menu drops down, as shown in Figure 16.1, earlier in this lesson.

4. In the Twitter area, enter your username and password.

5. Click to set or clear the **Send My Tumblr Posts to Twitter** check box.

    As the menu notes, you can toggle the option when posting.

6. Click the **Services** button to hide the menu.

7. Click the **Save + Close** button to save the changes and return to the Dashboard.

    When you post, you'll have the option of sending your post to Twitter as well, with the option to edit it before sending. Tumblr also converts photos to Twitter-friendly URLs. This is shown in Figure 16.4.

FIGURE 16.4 Tumblr gives you lots of options for cross-posting to Twitter.

Summary

In this lesson, you learned how to make Tumblr and Twitter work together as much as you like. You learned how to bring your own tweets, or your entire Twitter feed, into your tumblog. You also learned how to send your Tumblr posts to Twitter. Finally, you picked up some style tips on how to best use the services together.

Using Tumblr with Other Services

In this lesson, you learn how to flexibly combine Tumblr and several other services.

How Tumblr Plays Nice with Others

People who don't use services such as Tumblr have been known to wonder how people who do use them find the time. I have to admit that one of the scariest things I've ever heard is when someone I like told me he spends two hours a day on Facebook. If he's doing that, perhaps I should be, too, but where am I going to find two more hours a day?

In addition, Tumblr, unlike Twitter or Facebook, is not a service you're going to find nearly all of your real-world or online friends on. It's still a bit exclusive. Therefore, you might be tempted to combine various services so that an update to one goes to all the others.

However, as I've mentioned throughout this book, Tumblr has its own feel. If you want to use a Tumblr account as a kind of utility for your own purposes, that's fine—you can feed all sorts of stuff into and out of it. Also, you can have multiple tumblogs, one or more of which is for this kind of purpose. If you're creating a tumblog you want to share with people, though, be careful about how you wire things together. Tumblr is about quality, not quantity.

WARNING: You might be aware of what a "circular reference" is. For instance, in a spreadsheet program, you can easily have cell A1 depend on cell A2, which depends on cell A3, which depends on cell... A1! Your spreadsheet program should warn you when you try to do this.

However, you do not get a warning when you do the same thing with Tumblr and other blogging services. It would be nice, for instance, to have Tumblr, Twitter, and Facebook tied together so that an update to one of them updated the others, and you can do this with Tumblr's capabilities, third-party apps, or a combination.

However, it's easy to create a situation where each service is dependent on the other, and the results are—a scary word in computing—*undefined*. The practical effect can be that feeds stop working, or that you get the same post appearing multiple times in Tumblr, or in other services, or who knows what else!

If you start tying various services together and you have problems, start looking for circular references. You might find that you can fix the problem, or you might find you have to undo some of the connections you'd established. Maybe there should be a new blogging service just to fix this!

Keeping that in mind, there's still kind of a mad scientist quality to Tumblr's many interfaces to other services. This includes specific connections, such as to Twitter (see Lesson 16, "Using Tumblr with Twitter"), and Facebook, described in this lesson and more general RSS connections, also described in this lesson. There's a lot you can do—even if you have to go back and undo some of it later. Enjoy!

Feeding Your Tumblog into Facebook

In the early days of the Web, its founders wanted everyone to be a publisher on the Web, not just a consumer of other people's sites. Facebook brings this promise to life.

People love Facebook. It lets them have a life online that can be fully integrated with their real-world life—or as separate as they want it to be.

Tumblr makes a great front end to Facebook. The thought and care that people tend to put into Tumblr posts certainly makes them stand out among some of the routine updates found on Facebook. Creating a great tumblog can also teach you much of what you need to know to create a great Facebook page.

At the same time, people who are into Facebook aren't all that likely to leave it to visit your tumblog. When you bring your Tumblr posts into your Facebook page, they don't have to.

> TIP: If you want to impress Facebook early adopters, refer to it as "the Facebook," as it was originally known.

Follow these steps to send your Tumblr posts to Facebook:

1. If you aren't already logged in to Facebook, log in.

   Doing this first saves some confusion in setting up the connection between the services.

2. In Tumblr, choose **Account**, **Preferences**.

   The Preferences page displays.

3. Click the **Customize Your Blog** button.

   The Customize page displays.

4. Click the **Services** menu.

   The Services menu drops down.

5. In the Facebook area, click the **Setup** link.

   A Facebook window, Allow Access, displays, as shown in Figure 17.1.

6. Click **Allow**.

   A Facebook page displays that asks you to enter the address of your tumblog, as shown in Figure 17.2.

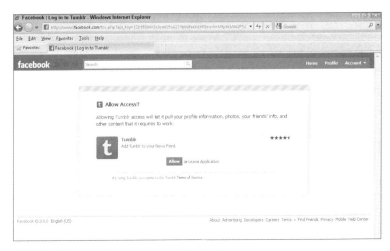

FIGURE 17.1 Ask Facebook to let Tumblr in.

FIGURE 17.2 Enter your tumlbog's URL.

7. Enter the URL of your tumblog and click the **Start Importing This Blog** button.

   A Request for Special Permissions displays, as shown in Figure 17.3, followed by two additional requests. If you've used

Facebook Connect with various web services, you have seen this
dialog previously.

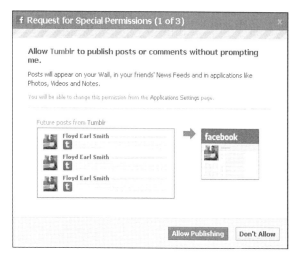

FIGURE 17.3   Give special permission for Tumblr.

8. In Facebook, click **Allow Publishing**; for the additional requests
   that display; click **Allow Access to Your Wall** and **Allow
   Constant Authorization** for ongoing updates.

   Facebook displays a success message. Note that you can click the
   link to disable and reconfigure the connection.

9. To change the settings, choose **Account**, **Application Settings**.

   A list of applications you used in the past month display, as
   shown in Figure 17.4. Note that the applications are in alphabeti-
   cal order.

10. Next to the Tumblr icon, click the **Edit Settings** link.

    Confirm or change your settings for Tumblr within Facebook.

11. Return to the Tumbler Customize page and click **Save** and **Close**.

    The changes will be saved.

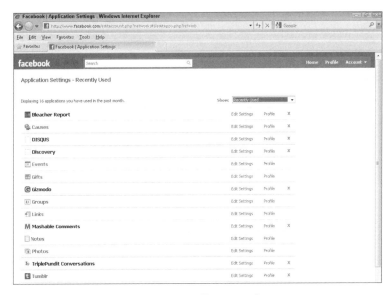

FIGURE 17.4   Success—but there's still more to do.

From here on, your Tumblr posts display in Facebook. Make sure to choose posts, or a tumblog, that's in keeping with your audience on Facebook as well as your audience on Tumblr.

Using Your Tumblog's RSS Feed

RSS stands for Really Simple Syndication. Although RSS is indeed really simple, the concept of syndication isn't.

RSS lets you get updates from all sorts of websites sent to you, either as email, or to a specialized front end, a "feed reader," or to a blog or other kind of publishing site. You don't have to surf the Web, at least for the sites you've subscribed to, because new information finds you.

There are, as a result, three generic types of RSS users, with many people fitting one of the types more or less exactly, and others representing a blend among them:

► **Never had it, never will**—These people don't like acronyms, or they don't like RSS, or they don't get it, and they don't bother with it.

► **Love it**—There are people who use RSS as a vital tool to keep up to date with what's happening on the parts of the Web that interest them, whether that's personally, professionally, or both.

► **Loved it, then left it**—Many people, including me, have signed up for RSS feeds to all sorts of things, found the resulting volume of input overwhelming, and dropped the whole thing.

This means that some people who "get it" or just push themselves to do it get a lot of use and value out of RSS. Others get little or none.

Regardless of your previous experience, or lack thereof, with RSS, it's a great tool for use with Tumblr. You can use RSS to export your Tumblr posts to a blog or other site, to capture other people's Tumblr posts to a blog or other site, to bring Tumblr posts into a feed reader, or to bring updates from various sites as a stream into your tumblog.

RSS is so capable that we can't describe everything you can do with it here. Instead, a brief description of how to set up each kind of use follows. Where you go from there is up to you.

You can often find the RSS feed for a site just by adding /rss to the end of the URL for the site. This works for your tumblog.

To access any RSS feed, including the feed for your tumblog, follow these steps:

1. Go to the home page of the site you want.

2. Change the URL so it's just the main address of the site, usually ending in .com, plus /rss.

   For instance, the RSS feed for my tumblog is at http://budsmith. tumblr.com/rss.

   Your blog will be displayed as a feed, as shown in Figure 17.5.

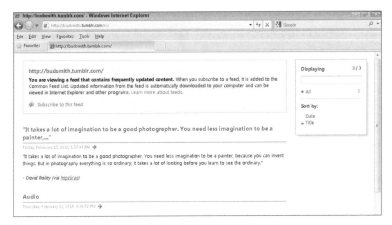

FIGURE 17.5   Your blog posts can be streamed as a feed.

3. To use either of these services, click the button for the service you want.

   The RSS feed is added to Google Reader or your Google homepage.

4. To use other services, start up the service and then enter the URL of the RSS feed into that service.

> TIP: You can find a good explanation of RSS and tools used for it at CNET. To learn more, visit http://reviews.cnet.com/4520-10088_7-5143656-1.html.

Importing RSS, Blog, and Other Feeds

Tumblr makes it easy to import many types of feeds in addition to Twitter, the subject of Lesson 16. You might need to experiment, however, to get them to display the way you want them to.

Here's a brief description of the types of feeds supported, as introduced in Lesson 16:

- ▶ **General website updates and news**—RSS (which is supported by many kinds of sites)

- ▶ **Blogs**—Blogger, LiveJournal, Vox, WordPress

- ▶ **"I like this" sites**—Del.icio.us, Digg

- ▶ **Video sites**—Vimeo, YouTube

> CAUTION: As mentioned in Lesson 16 with regard to Twitter, if you don't log into Tumblr or post directly to Tumblr fairly regularly, feed imports, such as the ones described here for Facebook, become inactive. "Fairly regularly" is a vague term, but if you haven't logged in to Tumblr for, say, a week or so, check your tumblog to see if your feeds are still working.

If the service you want to use isn't listed, there's a good chance you can access updates through RSS. Tumblr can support up to five feeds per account.

With regard to RSS, the capability to use so many feeds begs a question, though. Tumblr's "vibe" is all about quality, but RSS is mostly about quantity. How can you reconcile the two?

One way is to mostly bring in RSS feeds to a tumblog that you don't publicize and don't expect people to follow. This can even be an input from which you selectively copy and paste to your "public" blog.

You can also delete unwanted RSS-based posts. However, that means that anyone who follows your tumblog gets it all, good and bad.

The same is true, to a lesser extent, for other types of feeds. You might have a different purpose for your WordPress blog, for instance, than for your tumblog. If you use your WordPress blog as a feed, the results might not fit your tumblog.

Inputs from "I like this" sites are quite likely to be a good fit for your tumblog, though. As with a tumblog, your input to these kinds of sites reflects your individual taste and discretion—or, some people might think, lack thereof! Consider these "fit" factors carefully before importing an RSS feed or any other input.

Follow these steps to import an RSS feed:

1. In Tumblr, choose **Account**, **Preferences**.

   The Preferences page displays.

2. Click the **Customize Your Blog** button.

   The Customize page displays.

3. Click the **Services** menu.

   The Services menu drops down.

4. In the Automatically Import My area, use the pull-down menu to choose the type of input.

   The choices are RSS feed, Del.icio.us, Digg, Twitter, WordPress, Vox, Blogger, LiveJournal, Vimeo, and YouTube, as shown in Figure 17.6.

   For about half the feeds—RSS, WordPress, Vox, Blogger, and LiveJournal—you are asked to choose how to import the input: as Links, Links with Summaries, Text Without Titles, or Photos.

5. If you're asked in a pull-down menu how to import the input, choose one: As Links, Links with Summaries, Text Without Titles, or Photos.

   You might need to experiment with different types to see what works. One way to experiment is to import the same feed in several forms, and then compare the results in your tumblog to see which is best.

6. Enter the username, blog name, or URL that identifies your content.

7. Click the **Start Importing This Feed** button.

   A green box displays in the menu listing the new feed, along with any other feeds that you've set up that are currently in force.

8. To eliminate a feed, click the red X.

   The feed will be deleted.

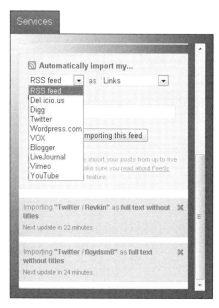

FIGURE 17.6   Tumblr importing is at your service(s).

Summary

In this lesson, you learned how to use Tumblr as a source for Facebook or any RSS client, and how to import RSS feeds, blog posts, video clips, and more into your tumblog. In addition, you learned how to manage the different approaches you can use in other web services with the particular approach you use in Twitter.

LESSON 18

Extending Tumblr with Comments, Goodies, and Apps

In this lesson, you learn how to extend Tumblr with comments, built-in apps from the Goodies menu, and third-party apps.

Tumblr Is Extensible

Tumblr is continually being improved and upgraded by the staff at Tumblr itself, by outside companies, and even by individuals.

Tumblr added an Application Programming Interface (API) early in its history. An API allows outsiders—and insiders—to create extensions to software that are guaranteed to work, as long as they follow the API's rules. Over time, an API is usually extended to make these extensions easier to create and more powerful.

Creating an API is a milestone for many kinds of technology for several reasons. First, it's hard to do. Slowing development of the core services to free up resources for creating and documenting those same services is a risk. The core software usually has to be improved, if not rewritten entirely, slowing everything further.

However, after the API is created, published, and proven to work, all sorts of third-party apps can be created—that is, if the core service still has enough momentum in the marketplace for developers to want to create software for it!

The iPhone is one example. Early in its life, Apple announced that there would be no API; it could be extended only by specialized web pages. Soon enough, Apple relented; an API was published; and the famous App Store was born. More than 100,000 apps later, it's a big reason why the iPhone is seen as a market leader.

In Tumblr's development, the third-party apps that use the Tumblr API serve as a kind of "minor leagues" for new ideas for Tumblr. All sorts of things get tried out as third-party apps. The best, most useful ideas are brought into Tumblr. This can happen by Tumblr buying the app and improving it, hiring in the app's creator or creative team, or stealing the idea and implementing it, in a more or less different form or any combination.

However, it has a good reputation, so Tumblr must be fairly nice people. This lesson shows you some of the recent additions brought into Tumblr, and third-party apps that are still outside, perhaps ready to be brought in.

Using Tumblr Community

Tumblr used to allow comments via a third-party app called Disqus. They even built a link to Disqus into Tumblr itself.

> NOTE: Confusingly, the term "API" is used as both a collective and a singular noun. It can mean, as used here, a collection of software interfaces, each with its own parameters. However, "API" can also be used for each of the specific functions within the overall, well, API. You can say, for instance, that "this version of the API is better than the last one because of the new APIs in it" and be correct, even if it also confusing.

As of early 2010, a lot of comment-type functionality has been added to Tumblr. This is made available through the Community menu in the Customize page.

Community allows you and, when you set things up a certain way, your tumblog visitors, to do some things that are similar to other blogging platforms—but, as you might expect, in a Tumblr-like style.

NOTE: The Tumblr community developed and grew without commenting by blog visitors for a while, and then only with Disqus third-party commenting, which was only so popular. Instead, every tumblog was potentially a comment on all the other tumblogs and on the service itself. Tumblr was a bit like an art gallery: Visitors were meant to admire the works on display, rather than comment on them. I expect it to be a long time before usage of comments-type features becomes common within Tumblr.

Follow these steps to enable community features in your tumblog; however, don't be surprised if the features are not heavily used by your site visitors, at least initially:

1. In Tumblr, choose **Account**, **Preferences**. The Preferences page displays.

2. Click the **Customize Your Blog** button.

   The Customize page displays.

3. Click the **Community** menu.

   The Community menu drops down, as shown in Figure 18.1.

4. For Replies, click one of the check boxes: Allow Replies from People You Follow or Allow Replies from People Following You for More Than Two Weeks.

   You can click both check boxes, but the first one makes the second one superfluous.

5. To enable questions, click the **Let People Ask Questions** check box. Change the Ask page title if you want by typing over the default choice, Ask Me Anything. Click the check box, Allow Anonymous Questions, if you want to allow anonymous questions.

   Questions are enabled with the settings you specify.

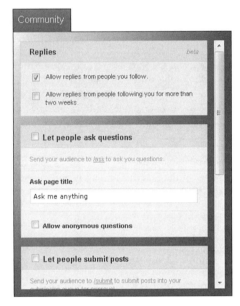

FIGURE 18.1   The Community menu gets people involved in a discussion about your tumblog.

6. Scroll down to see the Posts area, as shown in Figure 18.2.

7. To enable posts by visitors, click the **Let People Submit Posts** check box. Change the submission page title if you want, by typing over the default choice, Submit. You can also type in submission guidelines. Click the check boxes for each type of post you want to allow—text, photo, quote, link, and video. Finally, enter tags that you want submitters to be able to check for their posts, with the tag names separated by commas.

There are a lot of options here; experiment to get them right.

8. Click the **Community** menu to close it.

9. Click **Save** and **Close** to save your changes and exit the Customize page.

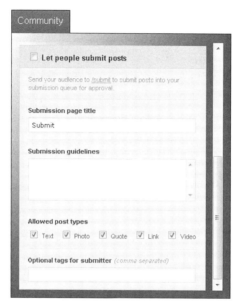

FIGURE 18.2   The Posts area in the Community menu lets visitors contribute directly to your tumblog.

Getting Goodies from Tumblr

Tumblr offers a set of goodies—extra functionality that may not be fully integrated into the rest of the Tumblr service—available from the Goodies page, shown in Figure 18.3.

However, at this writing, most of the functionality in Goodies is indeed integrated into the rest of Tumblr, but also displays in the Goodies menu. Here are the Goodies features as of this writing:

▶ **Bookmarklet**—A powerful capability that allows you to share content you find on the Web in your tumblog. When you hover over the **Share on Tumblr** button, a big green arrow displays. Drag the button up to the Bookmarks Bar of your browser, where it will reside. Repeat this by opening your Tumblr Goodies page in each browser that you want to have the capability in. (Bookmarklet might not work in Internet Explorer.)

FIGURE 18.3   Tumblr freely offers you Goodies.

▶ **Facebook app**—Described in detail in Lesson 17, "Using Tumblr with Other Services."

▶ **Mobile + email posting**—Described in Lesson 15, "Posting by Email, Phone, and Audio."

▶ **Publish to Twitter**—Covered in Lesson 16, "Using Tumblr with Twitter."

▶ **Third-party apps**—Listed in the next section of this lesson.

▶ **iPhone app**—A separate app for tumbling from your iPhone, which is explored Lesson 15.

▶ **Tumblet Dashboard Widget (Mac only)**—For posting text blurbs from your Mac desktop, shown in Figure 18.4. Click the **Download the Tumblet** link to download the Tumblet. The widget requires Mac OS 10.4, nicknamed Tiger, or later.

FIGURE 18.4 Here are even more Goodies.

Later versions of MacOS available at this writing, which the Tumblet also works on, include Mac OS 10.5, Leopard, and Mac OS 10.6, Snow Leopard. However, if you're a Mac fan, you probably have the Mac OS X versions list tattooed on that sensitive skin on the inside of your forearm.

▶ **Look up your contacts**—If you want to look up contacts from various online services and invite them to visit your tumblog and use Tumblr, click the **Find Your Contacts** link and follow the instructions.

▶ **Instant Message posting**—Mentioned in Lesson 6, "Creating a Text Post."

▶ **Embed your blog**—If you want to put your whole blog into another web page, copy and paste the code given on this part of the page into the HTML of the target web page. However, as the advisory note says, you should do this only if you're a trained professional—or at least a trained amateur—or can at least can borrow someone trained who will help you.

▶ **Call in Audio**—Covered in Lesson 12, "Posting Audio Clips." Quite a lineup! As you can see, you can use Tumblr as a kind of gathering point for one of your areas of interest or for all of them.

Using Tumblr Third-Party Apps

Tumblr has a set of third-party apps that it has "blessed" by putting them on a page of third-party apps in Tumblr itself. The Third-Party Apps page is accessed from the Goodies page, as described in the previous section. Figure 18.5 shows the Third-Party Apps page as it exists at this writing; this page is no doubt subject to change.

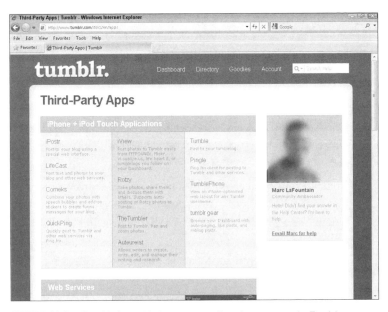

FIGURE 18.5 Tumblr has third-party apps listed on a page in Tumblr.

iPhone, iPod Touch, and iPad

Tumblr has several iPhone and iPod Touch applications, which should also run on the iPad. Following is a quick description:

- **iPostr**—iPostr is a web interface for posting to your tumblog, supporting all five types of Tumblr posts.

- **LifeCast**—As the name implies, LifeCast is for webcasting your life by posting to your tumblog. It currently supports text and photo posts.

- **Comeks**—A deliberate misspelling of "comics," this app allows you to easily add speech and thought bubbles to photographs, and then post to your tumblog.

- **QuickPing**—An iPhone app for simultaneously posting to Tumblr, Twitter, Facebook, Bebo, and other social networks. Keeping in mind what I said in the previous lessons about having a distinctive voice on Tumblr, there are times when this could be convenient indeed.

- **iView**—Quick posting for photos from various sources, including Flickr, the most popular web photo-hosting service, which is not directly supported by Tumblr.

- **Rotzy**—For sharing and discussing photos, you can autopost to Tumblr.

- **TheTumbler**—An app for posting to your tumblog that includes multiple post types and the ability to pan and zoom photos.

- **Auteureist**—This app is for writers to create, write, edit, research, and more; it includes a thesaurus and Tumblr support. This one should be great for the iPad, especially when used with its optional keyboard.

- **Tumble**—An alternative to the official iPhone Tumblr app mentioned previously and described in Lesson 15, Tumble is clean and simple, but doesn't do as much as the official app. It's fast, so you might want both apps.

- ▶ **Pingle**—Like QuickPing, this is an app for posting to multiple services.

- ▶ **TumblePhone**—This is a cool app that is a better way to look at tumblogs on your iPhone, with an iPhone-optimized layout.

- ▶ **tumblr gear**—This is a dashboard app that allows you to like and reblog posts, for example.

> TIP: Many iPhone developers are porting their apps to other types of cell phones to increase their reach. If you like one of these iPhone apps, but you use another kind of phone besides the iPhone, check the relevant app store for your phone. The app might have been ported to your phone, or something similar might be available. (See Tumblroid in the "Desktop + Mobile Applications" section in this lesson.)

Web Services

Web Services apps, shown in Figure 18.6, largely run in your browser. Some are related to the iPhone and iPod Touch apps listed previously; others are unique:

- ▶ **AlertThingy**—A kind of control panel for social networking, including Facebook, Twitter, Tumblr, and others.

- ▶ **Blip.fm**—A music sharing and discovery service that enables easy creation of audio posts for Tumblr.

- ▶ **Ping.fm**—Prominently represented in iPhone apps, Ping.fm is another control panel for social media, supporting not only web services such as Tumblr but also email, SMS, and more.

- ▶ **UpNext**—With the tagline, "What's UpNext in Your City?" UpNext is location-aware information, tailored to exactly where you are. Currently in beta and available only for Manhattan at this writing.

- ▶ **Tumblr YM**—Yahoo! Messenger can now be used to post to your blog.

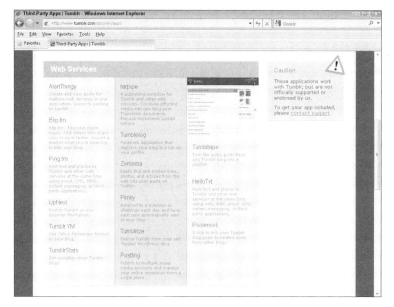

FIGURE 18.6   Tumblr's Web Services apps cover the waterfront.

▶ **TumblrStats**—Used for statistics about your Tumblr blog with pie charts and more.

▶ **Tarpipe**—Another control panel for social media, including photo services. Note: Tarpipe has UNIX roots; tar is a UNIX command for transferring data.

▶ **Tumblelog**—This is a version of the word "tumblog," but it's also the name of a Facebook application that brings the contents of your Tumblr blog into your Facebook profile.

▶ **Zemanta**—A service targeted for writers, Zemanta makes it easy to bring web content, such as photos, links, and so on, into your Tumblr posts; it is a kind of a dashboard for web content.

▶ **Plinky**—If you can't think of what to blog about, Plinky generates a question for you, and then helps you post the answer to Facebook, Twitter, Tumblr, and other services.

▶ **Tumblrize**—If you have a self-hosted WordPress blog—not a WordPress.com one—you can install Tumblrize, which makes it easy to post to your tumblog from WordPress.

▶ **Postling**—A control panel for your social media accounts, but it brings in recent content, not just outbound posts, allowing you to manage your online reputation.

▶ **Tumbltape**—Well regarded, this makes the audio posts from any tumblog into a playlist.

▶ **HelloTxt**—Lets you post text and photos to multiple services, such as Facebook, Twitter, and Tumblr, email, text messages, and more.

▶ **Psolenoid**—Ties your posts on multiple blogs to each other so that visitors to one can more readily see the others.

Desktop + Mobile Applications

Desktop + Mobile Applications for Tumblr, shown in Figure 18.7, is a hodgepodge of apps for non-iPhone smartphones and applications that run on your Mac, Windows, or Linux desktop:

▶ **Dial2Do**—This service lets you make text posts to Tumblr using your voice. If you've used voice recognition before, such as the automatic voicemail message transcription in Google Voice, you realize the possibilities for both productivity and hilarity here.

▶ **Jott**—Similar to Dial2Do, but has been around longer. Check both to see what each one costs.

▶ **Stumblr**—Posts to your tumblog from Symbian S60 devices, which makes up many of the mobile phones that aren't iPhones, Android phones, or BlackBerries.

▶ **TumblrSaver**—For Mac OS X, this is a screensaver that shows the latest and greatest tumblogs from the Tumblr Directory, known as The Wire.

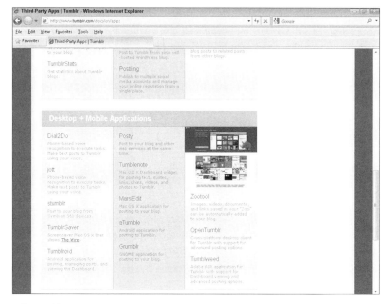

FIGURE 18.7   Tumblr has third-party apps listed on a page in Tumblr.

▶ **Tumblroid**—A highly capable mobile application for managing Tumblr from Android, it supports posting, management of posts, and Dashboard viewing. Compare it to aTumble, described later in this list.

▶ **Posty**—Posty is a tool for cross-posting to Tumblr and other blogging sites, all at the same time.

▶ **Tumblenote**—A Mac OS X Dashboard widget for posting text, photos, videos, and more; it does more than Tumblet, which is available from the Goodies menu described previously.

▶ **MarsEdit**—MarsEdit is a Mac application, not a web service, for posting to multiple blogs, including Tumblr.

▶ **aTumble**—Like Tumblroid, this is an Android application for posting to Tumblr.

▶ **Grumblr**—GNOME is an open-source desktop environment. If you use GNOME, you need Grumblr, which lets you post to your tumblog from GNOME. (I don't know if GNOME is in GALASKA.)

▶ **Zootool**—Zootool is a bookmarking service, and Zootool for Tumblr enables your Zootool bookmarks to be sent to your tumblog.

▶ **OpenTumblr**—OpenTumblr lets you post to your tumblog from Mac OS X, Windows, and Linux and includes advanced posting options.

▶ **Tumblweed**—Tumblweed enables you to view your Tumblr Dashboard and post to your tumblog with advanced options. It runs on Windows or Macintosh in the Adobe AIR environment, which you can download if you don't already have it.

Site Widgets and Browser Plug-Ins

Site Widgets and Browser Plug-Ins for Tumblr, shown in Figure 18.8, is a miscellany of apps that handle various functions:

▶ **Pikchur**—Think "picture." Update Facebook, Twitter, Tumblr, and other services with pictures or videos from your phone, via email or MMS.

▶ **n0nick's Verb**—For posting from a web page to your tumblog.

▶ **TumblrBadge**—This is JavaScript code to show your Tumblr posts in a web page, much like the Embed Your Blog code in the Goodies menu, described earlier in this lesson.

▶ **Tumblr Tag Cloud Generator**—Tag clouds are cool—they show your tags in, well, a cloud, with the most-used tags shown largest, and all are clickable. This might tell you more about what you're blogging about than you knew yourself.

▶ **Tumblr Post**—This Firefox add-on creates a "live" spot on your browser status bar. Drag and drop content to the spot to post it to your tumblog.

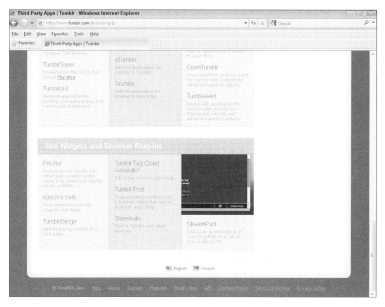

FIGURE 18.8   Tumblr has even more apps listed for you.

▶ **Shareholic**—A quick way to share links across services including Facebook, Twitter, Tumblr, Del.icio.us, and other services.

▶ **StreamPad**—StreamPad installs a little black bar at the bottom of your tumblog or other type of blog, such as WordPress, Blogger, and so on, that plays your audio posts.

Summary

In this lesson, you learned how to use Tumblr's Comments features, a relatively recent add-on, as well as Goodies and Apps, a steadily changing array of ways to improve your tumblog and access to it from your phone, the Web, or your computer desktop.

Index

Q-R

S

FREE Online Edition

Your purchase of **Sams Teach Yourself Tumblr® in 10 Minutes** includes access to a free online edition for 45 days through the Safari Books Online subscription service. Nearly every Sams book is available online through Safari Books Online, along with more than 5,000 other technical books and videos from publishers such as Addison-Wesley Professional, Cisco Press, Exam Cram, IBM Press, O'Reilly, Prentice Hall, and Que.

SAFARI BOOKS ONLINE allows you to search for a specific answer, cut and paste code, download chapters, and stay current with emerging technologies.

Activate your FREE Online Edition at
www.informit.com/safarifree

> **STEP 1:** Enter the coupon code: GJTVNCB.

> **STEP 2:** New Safari users, complete the brief registration form. Safari subscribers, just log in.

If you have difficulty registering on Safari or accessing the online edition, please e-mail customer-service@safaribooksonline.com